A River Runs through It

BRINGING A CLASSIC TO THE SCREEN

A River Runs through It

BRINGING A CLASSIC TO THE SCREEN

SCREENPLAY AND PREFACE
BY

RICHARD FRIEDENBERG

WITH AN INTRODUCTION
BY

ROBERT REDFORD

CLARK CITY PRESS
LIVINGSTON, MONTANA

WE RECOMMEND THAT ALL READERS TURN TO THE ORIGINAL NOVELLA:
A RIVER RUNS THROUGH IT AND OTHER STORIES, BY NORMAN MACLEAN,
AVAILABLE IN CLOTH AND TRADE PAPER FROM THE UNIVERSITY OF CHICAGO PRESS,
AND IN A MASS-MARKET EDITION FROM POCKET BOOKS.

PHOTOGRAPHS © 1992 BY:
FRANÇOIS DUHAMEL, SEVEN ARTS, PAGES 30, 41, 44, 47,
49, 50, 100, 123, 124, 139, 142, AND 143.
JOHN KELLY, PAGES 71, 74, 133, AND 135.
JOEL SNYDER, PAGES IV, X, 18, 36, 37, 57–60, 79, 86, 91, 97,
102, 104, 120, 128, 160, 164, 182, 187, AND 189.
DAVID STOECKLEIN, PAGES II–III, VIII, 3, 55, 72, 174, 178, AND 180.
MERIE W. WALLACE, SEVEN ARTS, PAGES 20, 22, 25, 27, 29, 32, 38, 56,
63, 106, 107, 108, 109, 144, 146, 151, 173, AND 184.
THE PHOTOGRAPHS ON PAGES 9, 10, 14, 15, 16, AND 17 ARE USED
WITH THE PERMISSION OF JEAN MACLEAN SNYDER.

CLARK CITY PRESS WISHES TO THANK THE FOLLOWING INDIVIDUALS AND INSTITUTIONS FOR
THEIR ASSISTANCE AND PATIENCE: JOEL SNYDER AND JEAN MACLEAN SNYDER, LOIS SMITH,
THERESA CURTIN, RICHARD FRIEDENBERG, CHRISTINE TAYLOR, ESTHER MARGOLIS,
BOB DATTILA, STEVE JACKSON, THE MONTANA HISTORICAL SOCIETY,
THE MIKE MANSFIELD LIBRARY, AND THE UNIVERSITY OF CHICAGO.

CLARK CITY PRESS
POST OFFICE BOX 1358
LIVINGSTON, MONTANA 59047

CONTENTS

A River Runs through It

Norman Maclean   /   Craig Sheffer

Paul Maclean   /   Brad Pitt

Jessie Burns   /   Emily Lloyd

Reverend John Maclean   /   Tom Skerritt

Clara Maclean   /   Brenda Blethyn

With appearances by Nicole Burdette, Stephen Shellen, Susan Traylor, Joe Gordon Levitt, Van Gravage, John and Madonna Reubens, David Creamer, Fred Oakland, Michael Cuditz, Rob Cox, Buck Simmonds, and William Hootkins.

Director of Photography   /   Philippe Rousselot

Screenplay   /   Richard Friedenberg

Executive Producer   /   Jake Eberts

Producer   /   Patrick Markey

Produced and Directed by
Robert Redford

Distributed by Columbia Pictures

From left: Brad Pitt, Robert Redford, Brenda Blethyn, Tom Skerritt, and Craig Sheffer.

In 1981, on a visit to Montana, I had a discussion about Western writers with my friend Tom McGuane. We debated the authenticity issue: living it and knowing it versus just loving it. Several names were thrown about—Wallace Stegner, Ivan Doig, A. B. Guthrie, Vardis Fisher—before McGuane suggested he could settle the question by having me read *A River Runs through It*, by Norman Maclean. "This is the real thing," he said.

I distrust such proclamations, but when I read the first sentence—"In our family there was no clear line between religion and fly fishing"—I thought I might be in for something. When I looked at the last line, I knew it. And when I'd finished reading the novella, I wanted to bring it to the screen.

What I had heard about Maclean indicated that he was not easy to approach. He was a phenomenon—a retired English professor at the University of Chicago who at age seventy-four wrote three stories and struggled to have them published. He was born in Montana at the turn of the century, and his early years were a blend of fighting, fishing, forestry, literature, and the strict discipline of his Presbyterian minister father. Maclean had achieved a position in the pantheon of revered writers with no nod to self-promotion or reviews, and he had very strict ideas regarding word and honor. Others had sought and failed to gain film rights to *River*; Maclean supposedly once turned down an actor who showed up to fish without a license.

I met Maclean in Sundance, Utah, in the mid-eighties to discuss the project. He was polite, courteous but wary, and surprisingly innocent. I decided that the best way to cut through the mythology that surrounded both of us would be to propose a plan that might strengthen our mutual trust. I would come to Chicago three times in six weeks, simply to talk about the project. He could ask questions; I would ask questions. I would tell him how I saw the story, and he could challenge and skewer that view as he liked. Above all, we would tell each other the truth. If at any point we didn't like the ways things were going, we could cut our losses.

I wasn't sure *River* could be made into a film. The story is slight, and relies heavily on Norman's voice as narrator. It is a maddeningly elusive piece, dancing away from the reader like the boxer Norman had once been, coming in fast to whack you between the eyes with the beauty of its language, or in the solar plexus with the depth of its emotion.

But when our sessions ended six weeks later, I was sure I wanted to make the film, and Norman was almost sure he could let it go. I offered a final incentive: I would show him the first draft as it was being composed, and if he didn't like it he could pull the plug on the project. If Norman liked the script, he would step away and let me make the film without interference.

Three years and several drafts later, I came to Montana again, this time to film *A River Runs through It*. Norman had died a few months earlier, and I'm not sure he would have ever borne the shift from the privacy of pen and page to the very public business of film. His book was a great challenge; I'd like to think we saw eye to eye on much, and that the end result reflects that unison.

—Robert Redford

Fly fishing on Rattlesnake Creek, Montana, 1903.

I was delighted when my agent called with the news that Robert Redford wanted me to write the script for his next film—he was an Academy Award–winning director, and the film would be an independent production, not a big studio film. I soon received a slim novella entitled *A River Runs through It*, by Norman Maclean. It was beautiful. It was profound. It was moving. And my heart sank: it was not a movie.

A movie can't be, and shouldn't try to be, a book. You can't put a movie down in the middle or reread a paragraph to better understand it. You can't make up the characters' faces in your mind, or hear their thoughts, their backgrounds, past lives and loves, families, ancestors, anecdotes. And you can't sneak to the last page to see what happens. The audience has to understand scene one before it is gone forever, replaced by scene two. The twists and turns and huge lists of characters so common in novels need to be sorted, selected, rejected, in order to make a compelling, comprehensible screenplay—simple but not emotionally simple.

But the problem facing me was not one of condensation. *A River Runs through It* is only 104 pages long, fifty-two of which consist of detailed passages about fly fishing. That left me barely a wisp of a story, evocative and elegant though it was, and the fact that it was told by Norman's character compounded my difficulties. Though this device works admirably in the novella, where Norman's graceful description and dry wit carry us deep into the lives of his family, the distance the narrator maintains from the story, in time and in emotion, renders much of the language unusable. The Norman in the novella is a settled man, married, a father in the midst of comfortable success, far removed from the curiosity and anguish of youth. The actual story is propelled by Paul's anguish and darkness in a youth he can't leave.

I faced a beautiful book that I could only see as a movie about a middle-aged professor explaining the sadness of his brother's life, interspersed with fifteen-page exegeses on the art and religion of fly fishing. My task, finally, was to recreate the book's magic without having the benefit of the book's methods. The key, I was convinced, lay in research. *River* is, after all, a reminiscence, fictionalized to a degree, but still the memory of Norman's life, and I imagined that there existed many more stories from his memory that could add dimension and substance to a script.

When I flew to Chicago to visit him in 1988, Norman was quite ill and frail and could spend little time with me. But his daughter and son-in-law, Jean and Joel Snyder, were full of information, insights, explanation. The world of Norman Maclean in the early part of our century began to take shape. I travelled next to Missoula, Montana, Norman's boyhood home. I met his contemporaries, and at last hit on the piece of research that lit my flame: A high school yearbook from 1920. There was Norman, impossibly young, a running back on the football team, a public speaker, a poet, a boy most likely to succeed. I finally realized that to make "my" Norman dimensional I needed to put him back in the twenties when he returned from college, uncertain of his future and ashamed of his uncertainty. It was the time when he learned he'd been accepted into the graduate program at the University of Chicago, the time when he met and wooed Jessie.

If I also pushed Paul's crisis back into that same period, I could create the story I sought—the rise of Norman from uncertainty to purpose, from boyhood to manhood, set against Paul's downward arc, from competent journalist to lost artist, from worldly lover to stubborn child, unable to mature, beautiful on the river but damned in life. To me that was a story a film could tell. A movie.

Those who loved the book might feel betrayed by the changes made, but Norman himself fictionalized his life. And as I worked my way slowly through the screenplay, I kept in mind Norman's own advice:

> "You like to tell true stories, don't you?" [my father] asked, and I answered, "Yes, I like to tell stories that are true."
>
> Then he asked, "After you have finished your true stories sometime, why don't you make up a story and the people to go with it?
>
> "Only then will you understand what happened and why."

In a larger sense the issue is not whether I changed the book, but whether I retained its intention and the spirit of the book. If I violated Norman's original intention, I failed. If I managed to keep *his* spark alive, despite the changes, then I succeeded.

At the time of Norman Maclean's birth in 1902 his father John Maclean was older than Montana, a vast wilderness of plains and mountains and deep forests, dotted by mud-streeted towns through which the great rail lines stitched

Missoula at the turn of the century.

a tenuous thread of civilization. In Missoula, where the Maclean family settled in approximately 1906, cowboys, miners, lumberjacks, free-speech
Wobblies and railroad workers mingled on Front Street, all lured by whores'
"cribs" and swinging-door saloons. Train robberies were still the order of the
day, as were public hangings. But the wildness of the early years was fast
wearing away: The Indian tribes were no longer a threat to white expansion
(Chief Charlo posed for a photo in Missoula's first car), the University of
Montana was going strong, and as early as 1902 the well-organized Women's
Club got an ordinance passed that outlawed spitting on the city sidewalks.

This dichotomy in the fabric of Missoula—the wild West against the on-
slaught of the twentieth century—was a determining influence on the young
lives of Norman Maclean and his brother Paul, born in 1906. Norman called
his youth "schizophrenic": while he conformed to the religious and intellectual atmosphere of his father's circle, he was at the same time busy becoming
a hard-drinking, street-fighting, profane Westerner—"a tough choirboy."
This schizophrenia stayed with Norman throughout his life, and marked his
writing style.

Painted on one side of our Sunday School wall were the words, God Is Love. We always assumed that these three words were spoken directly to the four of us in our family and had no reference outside, which my brother and I soon discovered was full of bastards, the number increasing rapidly the farther one gets from Missoula, Montana.

The Reverend Maclean fostered this educated toughness. In his study hung a plaque that read, "No One Shall Touch Me With Impunity." Although he was committed to brotherly love, he turned a blind eye on his boys' fighting, only getting angry if they lost.

The reverend, born in Dalhousie, New Brunswick, was not a native Westerner—hardly anyone was at the time—but he exemplified the best of the tough, self-reliant pioneers that settled the American West. He fished; he hunted; he built a cabin at Seeley Lake with his own hands from logs he cut himself and floated across the lake, all the while quoting snatches of poetry from Wordsworth and Robert Burns. Unlike many Presbyterian ministers of the time, he fashioned gentle, charming sermons, working the whole week on each one, editing until the words flowed like the poetry he loved. His parishioners were slightly in awe of the educated, dapper, poetic but distant minister.

The reverend only concerned himself with the minds of his flock, and left their day-to-day dramas to his wife. Clara Maclean was raised in the wilds of Manitoba and believed in hard work and family, and in the nineteenth-century version of a woman's place. She stood quietly and steadfastly behind her husband, always referring to him in public as Dr. Maclean. She tended her husband's flock, sat up with them when they were ill, listened to their endless problems, ran charities for the reservation tribes, raised her boys, and kept house in an era of brooms and scrub brushes and hand laundry. Norman recalled no complaint or even discussion of this gruelling work.

If the minds of the parishioners were John Maclean's concern at church, at home the minds of his children were of paramount importance. His purpose in life was to teach, to try to raise his boys through constant struggle, both intellectual and artistic, toward the understanding of God's rhythms. The question of what Norman or Paul should do with their understanding was left up to them. The reverend meddled very little in his sons' lives after their daily lessons, rarely mentioning the peccadillos that came to him via the church grapevine. The Macleans, in fact, spoke little to each other of significant fam-

John and Clara Maclean with Norman and Paul in approximately 1915.

ily issues. As Norman said, late in his life, "People who love each other don't snoop. Snooping destroys love, which is a matter of infinite acceptance." John Maclean would have seconded that theory. The love he felt for his family, though undoubtedly strong, was simply not demonstrated. The one thing he most hated was leaving town on the train, because then he would be forced to kiss his wife good-bye in public.

World War I changed Missoula forever, as it changed all of rural America. Until 1915 the majority of Americans lived in the country—really country— but with the onset of war the inexorable movement of population to urban centers began. Missoula paved its streets, installed an electric railway, built new bridges and municipal buildings. But the most singular event of the period was the election to Congress in 1916 of Jeannette Rankin, the first woman to serve in a country that still did not allow women to vote. One of

Paul Maclean, age twenty-three.

her first acts in the House, and certainly her most notorious, was the "no" vote she gave to the U.S. entering World War I. But when the country went to war, Missoula followed with extraordinary vigor, sending 25 percent more men to the conflict than the national quota required. In all, 960 men from Missoula County died overseas, and the state of Montana suffered the highest per capita loss of any state in America.

Norman was too young to join the grim adventure, but duty still called him. He replaced the drafted woodsmen, joining the U.S. Forest Service at the tender age of fifteen. He stood lonely watches amidst storms and rattle-snakes, fought forest fires, and handled one end of a crosscut saw, while during the school year he continued to excel in poetry and public speaking.

Paul's life took a different turn. He never joined the Forest Service, nor thought of himself as a writer. He was a star athlete in high school, and a lady-killer later—and, it seems fairly certain, he was always in a sense the favored son. To his mother Paul was the only man who ever hugged her in public and damned the consequences. To his father Paul was, inexplicably and undoubtedly, a master with the rod and reel.

Fly fishing was as close to a religious act for the reverend as anything he did in life. He believed that in fly fishing as well as in religion one could attain grace only by constant struggle. Yet here was a boy who seemed to become an artist on the river with almost no effort. While Norman patiently and obediently followed his father's strict instructions, Paul soared, creating, inventing, surpassing the other two men. While Norman's style evolved directly from his father's—delicate, close-in, accurate—Paul, the taller of the two, broke away and used his tremendous strength to develop distance. He was blessed with perfect timing, and seldom if ever missed a fish, no matter how long the cast. It must have sorely puzzled the reverend, but also most certainly filled him with awe.

Fly fishing at that time—the teens and twenties—and in that place had to have been a wonder and a delight, but only for the intrepid. Few roads led into the wilderness of such river systems as the Blackfoot, the Clearwater, the Swan. Fishermen had to hike in, rarely crossing the path of another human being for days at a time. The flies used during that time were large, small flies not arriving in the West for some time to come. They were made with materials at hand, even the plumes from a mother's hat. Creative flytiers, like the Reverend Maclean, designed their own patterns to address the specific insect hatches of the area, and gave them names like Brown-hackle Peacock, Royal Coachman, Silver Doctor, Professor, and Ginger Quail. Fishermen used bamboo rods and silk line with catgut leaders, and hauled heavy cane creels that they filled with their limit of twenty-five trout a day. Catch-and-release fishing was unheard of. All the fish caught were shared by family and friends, fried up by the women on their hot wood stoves.

Norman and Paul would start off together on a fishing expedition, driving as far as they could overland in the reverend's high-wheeled Dodge, then hiking miles to their favorite holes. More often than not Paul fished alone once they reached their destination, spending the day far from even his brother's company. Solitude was essential for his chosen art. The brothers preferred rough water, so cold that when their aged hobnail logging boots soaked through, their entire lower legs went numb and stayed that way all day. Hip boots were considered a foolish affectation—wild water could easily fill them and drown the fisherman.

The staff of the Missoulian *in 1908.*

In the choice of higher education the two boys again differed. Norman, being the elder son of a Scot, had always been expected to carry the Maclean banner forth to great intellectual success. He chose Dartmouth, far away from the life he loved in Missoula. Though he met with quick success, and was asked by the faculty to teach classes, he "wasn't big on rich eastern guys with names that always had numbers after them like the kings of England . . ." He made a specialty of "outdrinking the bastards, beating them at cards, and then, since they were indisposed, taking their dates back to their guest houses—always by circuitous routes that left plenty of time for looking at the moon."

Paul started college at the University of Montana, and though he transferred to Dartmouth upon Norman's urging, he did not accumulate enough credits and was forced to finish his math at Montana. One professor there, a heavy drinker and a socialist, exercised a profound influence on Paul, and the two of them "drank their way through calculus, cursing the big mining companies all the way," recalled Norman, who remembered one of the math problems Paul received:

If a swine of an Anaconda capitalist can sweat thirteen hours out
of a copper miner each day for six days in a row, and if the bastard
can get the miner to haul a ton and a half of copper ore each hour
of the working day, and if the miner has only ten minutes to eat
his lunch and can't take time out to piss, then how long will . . .

Paul finished the course with an A. He decided on a career in journalism to
fight the social injustice of the day, injustice that he believed was largely
brought on by Anaconda Copper and Mining. This monolithic company
unfortunately controlled virtually every newspaper Paul worked for in
Montana.

When Norman stepped off the Northern Pacific after his final year at Dartmouth, he found a city wrapped in "normalcy." By the roaring part of the
twenties, Missoula had succeeded in becoming a mainstream American
town. Its red-brick buildings, macadam streets, solid wooden homes, and
fleets of black Model Ts differed little from those in towns across the country.
Jazz bands played in the park. Women's hair and skirts were shorter. Liquor
was illegal but easily located—the cribs and saloons were gone but had been
quietly replaced with speakeasies. Missoula's Chinese and blacks weren't
served, and Indians were not allowed to live within the city limits.

Not long after Norman returned, he met Jessie Burns. She was the eldest
of seven children, all born and raised in the tiny hamlet of Wolf Creek, Montana, which, as Norman described, "is in a narrow canyon that barely has
enough room for the creek, a dirt road and the train tracks." Jessie's father,
John Burns, was a likeable Irishman who married a Scot, Florence McLeod,
and proceeded to run a store that barely scraped along. What Jessie absorbed
from her poor, unruly, not-unhappy family was a tolerance for people, something that the Macleans never had in great quantity.

Jessie was a flapper, not by peer pressure, but by true nature, more akin to
Paul than to Norman. She was an adventurer, a daredevil, living her youth at
the right time for women to begin realizing their power. She could vote,
dance the Charleston, drink and drive as hard as any man. And she could
stand up to Norman's toughness, something few people ever managed. Yet
she saw in Norman a spark of serious, quiet romanticism that led her to
marry the son of a stiff and proper Presbyterian family.

During the months he spent wooing Jessie, Norman struggled to become
a professional writer. He'd actually completed a novel at Dartmouth, but the
boarding house he lived in burned to the ground, and his two years' work was

Jessie with her father John Burns and brother Ken; their Wolf Creek grocery is in the background.

lost. Back home, the reverend allowed him to flounder on for some time. Then, as Norman put it, "My father, who never spoke to me about the way I ran my life, looked me straight in the eyes and said, 'Norman, I don't think you have grown in the last two years.' And I looked at myself and had to agree that I had become a very handy man with a deck of cards and nothing else."

Norman gratefully accepted an offer from the University of Chicago to teach literature while finishing his Ph.D. He married Jessie and moved away from Montana, away from his childhood, really. In Chicago he became a re-sponsible, established adult, with a house, children, and a career.

Paul would never have or seek any of these signs of stability. He eventually joined Norman in Chicago, but each summer he and Norman would come to Montana to renew their bond with "the natural side of God's order," and every summer Paul's casting ability grew. Perhaps it was this extraordinary ability that kept Norman, as well as his father and mother, from bringing up their worries about Paul, who kept the curtain tightly closed over his life.

Jessie Burns Maclean.

Norman recalled only the slightest hints of fighting, whoring, drinking, gambling, usually couched in odd stories or jokes. Thus the family remained unsure of Paul's problems, unsure even that he had problems, and were tentative in approaching him.

> And we were also hesitant because we looked clumsy when we tried to help, and he looked like what he was, an artist whose Scottish pride was offended by a clumsy offer of help.

In 1938, Paul was beaten to death in an alley in Chicago. The family never knew whether it was a mugging, a fight, or the payment of some debt he owed. They were never to know any more at all about Paul. Norman said, "In the end all we knew—really knew—about him was that he was beautiful and dead and we had not helped." The Macleans were not a family that spent time in deep discussions of Paul's death, and after a certain point it was not

Norman lecturing at the University of Chicago.

mentioned again. Norman kept the pain and guilt locked inside himself, not even sharing it with Jessie.

Norman's life went on in solidity and brilliance. He became one of the most revered teachers at the University of Chicago, known for his dry wit, his toughness, and the C's that he felt almost everyone richly deserved. The reverend and Clara retired to a reservation in northern Montana, where they ran a mission until John's death at the age of seventy-nine.

It was not until years later, after Jessie's untimely death from emphysema in 1968, after his two children were grown and married, after he finally retired from the university, that Norman began to write a small book about religion and fly fishing in the Montana of his youth, and about the death of his brother Paul. For the first time, he faced the pain and turned it into words. And that seemed to release the sadness that had by then become so deeply a part of him. He had stood dry-eyed at the police station, at the coroner's inquest, at the funeral. Now, almost four decades later, as he read the beautiful, hopeful ending of *A River Runs through It* to his daughter, he began to cry for the first time.

"The past is everywhere around me," he said almost at the end of his life. "I came to terms with it by making it into art."

—Richard Friedenberg

Paul and Norman Maclean in 1913.

Vann Gravage and Joe Gordon Levitt
as Paul and Norman Maclean.

Fade in:

1. *EXT. COUNTRY ROAD—LATE AFTERNOON—PRESENT DAY. A car stops on the side of the road above a wide, dark river, and* NORMAN MACLEAN, *age seventy-five, emerges from it. He's dressed in old and practical clothes, well-oiled leather boots, a warm shirt, an obviously cherished, shapeless hat, pierced with dozens of beautiful flies. He opens the trunk of his car and gently removes a fishing rod, holding it out straight before him, eyeing along its length. The polished bamboo glows in the early light. The tip vibrates with the old man's pulse. Satisfied, he starts slowly down the slope to the river. A* NARRATOR'S VOICE *begins. It is Norman's, old and thin but still beautiful, a voice used to reciting poetry and telling stories.*

NARRATOR

In our family, there was no clear line between religion and fly fishing. We lived at the junction of great trout rivers in western Montana, and our father was a Presbyterian minister and a fly fisherman who tied his own flies and taught others. He told us about Christ's disciples being fishermen and we were left to assume, as my brother and I did, that all first-class fishermen on the Sea of Galilee were fly fishermen and that John, the favorite, was a dry-fly fisherman.

As he speaks, Norman's arm begins a motion, lifelong, almost unconscious, a small arc above his head, back and forth, the rod picking up speed, the end whipping; and finally he lets it go. The line snakes out, a bright flash against the dark water, and hits, fly first, soundless and perfect.

2. *EXT. RIVER—MISSOULA, MONTANA, 1912—DAY. (Still period photos) Another river runs through the center of a small, dusty town. Above its banks, in a block of plain wooden buildings, stands a new brick church. The street running past it is dirt. Horses hitched to carriages stand out front.*

[19]

Paul, Clara (Brenda Blethyn), and Norman listen to the reverend's sermon.

NARRATOR

It is true that one day a week was given over wholly to religion.

3. INT. CHURCH—DAY.

NARRATOR

On Sunday mornings my brother Paul and I went to Sunday school and then to morning services to hear our father preach, and in the evenings to Christian Endeavor, and afterwards to evening services to hear our father preach again.

REVEREND *(v.o.)*

Poverty is an evil thing and bitter when it shuts the door of op-
portunity to the higher possibilities and privileges of life. There
are multitudes of our fellow men toiling against the rough seas of
penury and want. Their shoulders are bent to the task and their
hearts are despairing . . .

At the pulpit the REVEREND MACLEAN *stands, a slim, elegant man of forty-eight, in
a tailored robe. He is not a hellfire preacher. His voice is soft, his sermon a story,
charming and magnetic to the faithful who sit attentively in their Sunday best.*

REVEREND

. . . and no one seems to care. But wait a little till I tell you. There
is one yonder who sees and cares and would be your help. It is he
who when on earth had nowhere to lay his head, but who is now
crowned with glory and immortality. He would come into the
poor man's life, saying—"Come unto me all ye that labor and are
heavy laden and I will give you rest. Take my yoke upon you and
learn from me, for I am meek and lowly of heart and ye shall find
rest for your souls, for my yoke is easy and my burden is light."
The poor without Christ are of all men most miserable, but the
poor with Christ are princes and kings of the earth . . .

In the front pew his WIFE *watches. She is thirty-eight, with a fair English complex-
ion.* NORMAN, *a slight, dark, ten-year-old, sits beside her, trying dutifully to pay attention.* PAUL, *fair-haired, eight, leans against her other side, his eyes glazing, his
body rocking back and forth.*

*4. EXT. THE BIG BLACKFOOT RIVER—DAY. Norman and Paul walk with their father
along the wild, beautiful river.*

The reverend (Tom Skerritt) with Norman and Paul.

NARRATOR

In the afternoon we would walk with him while he unwound between services. He almost always chose a path along the Big Blackfoot, which we considered our family river. And it was there he felt his soul restored, and his imagination stirred.

The Reverend picks up a rock, explaining, as the boys study the fossilized raindrops on it, touching them with their grubby fingers:

REVEREND

Long ago rain fell on mud and it became rock. A half billion years ago. But even before that, beneath the rocks are God's words. They came first. Listen.

NARRATOR

. . . And if Paul and I listened very carefully, all our lives, we might hear those words.

The boys listen to the SOUNDS *of the* RIVER. *The ripples and eddies and waves of the river flow past, bringing us to:*

4A. EXT. MANSE—DAY. *The three are in front of the house, preparing for a fishing lesson on land.*

NARRATOR

Even so, in a typical week of our childhood Paul and I probably received as many hours of instruction in fly fishing as we did in all other spiritual matters.

As a Scot and a Presbyterian my father believed that man by nature was a damned mess and had fallen from an original state of grace, and that only by picking up God's rhythms were we able to regain power and beauty. Unlike many Presbyterians, he often used the word "beautiful."

The Reverend pulls on a thin glove and buttons it, while the boys watch, impressed by his style. Then he holds his rod out straight. The boys imitate him. We HEAR *his* VOICE, *lecturing under the narration.*

NARRATOR

Then he would say, "Casting is an art that is performed on a four-count rhythm between ten and two o'clock." My brother and I would have preferred to start learning how to fish by going out and catching a few, omitting entirely anything difficult or technical in the way of preparation that would take away from the fun . . .

The Reverend starts an old wooden metronome and begins casting, the boys following with difficulty.

NARRATOR

. . . but it wasn't by way of fun that we were introduced to our father's art. If our father had had his say, nobody who did not know how to fish would be allowed to disgrace a fish by catching it.

The scene becomes a SERIES OF IMAGES—*the boys' concentrated faces, a hand holding a rod, the Reverend's gloved hand gently correcting, the lines arcing over the yard. We see a progression in the boys' abilities.*

NARRATOR

So my brother and I learned to cast Presbyterian style, on a metronome. It was my mother's metronome, which Father had taken from the top of the piano.

Then Mother appears, nervously watching the metronome as it teeters on the dock until she can't stand it.

MOTHER

Stop!

The three men turn in surprise. Silently, Mother holds a hand out. While Norman and the Reverend look guiltily away, Paul takes the metronome and hurries it to her. The Reverend waits a respectful beat as she turns back up the path, then:

REVEREND

And . . .

He starts clapping the four-count rhythm with his cupped hands and the boys begin the lesson once more.

Dissolve to:

5. EXT. *DOCK*—DAY. *The three continue their lessons on a pond, the boys improved.*

The reverend gives Norman and Paul a casting lesson.

NARRATOR

My father was very sure about certain matters pertaining to the universe. To him, all good things, trout as well as eternal salvation, came by grace and grace comes by art, and art does not come easy.

6. *INT. HOUSE—STUDY—MORNING. Norman reluctantly descends the staircase, a sheet of paper in hand, and walks the dark hall to the Reverend's study.*

So it was with my formal education as well. Each weekday from nine A.M. till noon, while my father worked on his Sunday sermon and my mother tended the flock, I attended the school of the Reverend Maclean.

Norman waits while his father works on a sermon with deep concentration. Norman's eyes wander to a plaque on the wall behind the Reverend. It reads: "No One Will Touch Me With Impunity," and is surrounded by angry carved Scotch thistles. Finally the Reverend looks up. Norman holds out the paper. Automatically, the Reverend takes a thick red pencil from a jar, obviously made by one of the boys, and begins to read the theme entitled, "Grace." Norman's shoulders slump in expected defeat as the Reverend marks ruthlessly sentence after sentence. At the door, little Paul watches unseen, taking it in, his blond curls, caught by the morning sun, the only brightness in the dour, book-lined room.

NARRATOR

He taught nothing but reading and writing, and, being a Scot, believed that the art of writing lay in thrift.

The Reverend finishes. Norman stiffens as his father hands back the paper and says, not unkindly:

REVEREND

Half as long.

7. INT. NORMAN'S ROOM—DAY.

NARRATOR

So while my friends attended Missoula elementary I stayed home and learned to write the American language.

Norman sits at his desk working over the red-marked theme, his face set, determined. Paul appears, barely seen behind the door.

Norman watches as the reverend corrects his essay.

7A. INT. STUDY—DAY. The red pencil rises, stops above the page. Norman tenses. Then the pencil descends, marking quickly, expertly, and the Reverend speaks those dire words again, softly, almost sorrowfully.

REVEREND

Again. Half as long.

7B. INT. NORMAN'S ROOM—DAY. He sits hunkered over a new piece of paper, struggling to solve his father's critique. Paul appears at the door and leans against it, watching cautiously, carefully, as Norman crosses out his latest sentence, ripping the paper. A tear drops onto it. Norman grits his teeth, refusing to cry. Paul's mouth compresses in empathy.

8. INT. STUDY—DAY. Once more Norman stands before his father watching the red pencil poised above the sheet, ready to attack the theme, now reduced to a single paragraph.

REVEREND *(smiles)*

Good. Now throw it away.

ANGLE—WASTEPAPER BASKET. With immense satisfaction, Norman crumples the theme into a tight ball and fires it into the Indian wicker basket.

9. EXT. REAR OF HOUSE—DAY. Norman bursts outside, but Mother calls:

MOTHER

Norman, wait for your brother . . . !

NARRATOR

However, there was a counterbalance to my father's stern system: in the afternoon, I was set free, untutored and untouched until supper, to learn on my own the natural side of God's order.

And Norman dutifully waits as little Paul hastily gathers up his fishing gear and runs out to join him. Both boys dash off into the wilderness.

NARRATOR

And there could be no better place to learn than the Montana of my youth. It was a world with dew still on it, more touched by wonder and possibility than any I have since known.

10. EXT. WOODS AND FIELD—DAY. (Montage) The boys run in the primeval forest, fish, swim with friends, watch Indians at the river.

The boys run to the river.

NARRATOR

But it was a tough world, too. Even as children we understood
that, and admired it.

*11. EXT. THE TOWN—DAY. (Montage) A rough frontier town with horses, saloons,
six-guns, liquor and gambling. Paul does a cootchy-coo dance for a gaggle of whores,
who laugh and do it back. The boys pull down the pants of a drunk. The boys watch
a real, frightening fight.*

NARRATOR

And, of course, we had to test it.

*11A. EXT. ROAD—ANOTHER LOCATION—DAY. Norman and Paul spar, Norman
in a stand-up, bare-knuckle pose, instructing, Paul trying to imitate him, both laughing, enjoying themselves.*

Robert Redford gives some tips to Joe Gordon Levitt and Vann Gravage.

11B. EXT. TOWN—ANOTHER LOCATION—DAY. Norman is in a real fight with another boy. They are swinging hard, all form gone. Norman's nose is bleeding. Paul and the other boys cheer them on.

NARRATOR

I knew I was tough because I had been bloodied in battle . . .

Suddenly, little Paul leaps from the sidelines into the fray like a wild animal, yelling, swinging. The others grab him and pull him back, holding on while he shouts and twists. Norman and his opponent both stop, looking at Paul in surprise.

NARRATOR

Paul was different. His toughness came from some secret place inside of him. He simply thought that he was tougher than anyone alive.

[30]

12. *INT. N.D. C.U. Paul's face, quiet and composed, head bowed.*

13. *INT. DINING ROOM—MORNING. Now we can see that he is sitting at the break-fast table, before him an untouched bowl of oatmeal. The family, long finished, is waiting for him to begin eating. But he doesn't move. The moment stretches, tense. Finally, quiet but strong:*

                    REVEREND

This morning you *will* eat the oatmeal, Paul.

There is no response. The little boy doesn't move. The Reverend sighs, ironic.

                    REVEREND

Men have been eating God's oats for a thousand years. It is not the place of an eight-year-old boy to change that tradition.

Norman and Mother stare at Paul, willing him to eat. Nothing. The Reverend's face reddens.

                    REVEREND

Do you *hear* me?

Nothing.

                    REVEREND

SPEAK!!

Paul's lips move. The Reverend jumps.

                    REVEREND

What?
        (to Mother) What did he say?

Paul and the uneaten oatmeal.

MOTHER

He said he doesn't like it.

At a loss, the Reverend opens his mouth, but can think of no response. Unable to stand it another minute, Mother grabs some dishes and hurries into the kitchen. Norman waits one beat, then takes some more dishes and runs after her, leaving the Reverend to stand staring at his little son. Finally, drained:

REVEREND

Grace will not be said until your bowl is clean.

He walks out, leaving Paul alone.

14. *INT.* DINING ROOM—DAY. *Midday light floods in.* FOOTSTEPS *can be* HEARD *in other rooms,* CHILDREN'S VOICES *outside, happy, laughing. But Paul remains as still as a statue, bowed over the oatmeal as if praying.*

[32]

15. *INT. STUDY—DAY. At the same time the Reverend sits bowed in exactly the same attitude over his work, speaking his sermon to himself as is his habit. The mantel* CLOCK TICKS. *Neither moves. It is a test of will.*

16. *INT. DINING ROOM—DAY. The Reverend appears, sits at the head of the table. Hearing him, Mother pokes her head out. He doesn't look up as she and Norman assume their seats. Another beat, then, very quietly:*

REVEREND

Grace.

The four kneel beside their chairs, eyes closed, hands clasped as the Reverend murmurs grace. Norman peers, impressed and unsettled, at Paul, his cherubic face giving no indication of the victory he has won. Above the family, on the bare table, the bowl of oatmeal sits untouched.

REVEREND

O God, who art rich in forgiveness, grant that we may always hold fast the good things which we receive from Thee, and as often as we fall into sins, may be raised up by repentance, through Thy mercy. Amen.

17. *EXT. THE RIVER—DAY. Paul sits entranced as Norman tells a story with great drama.*

NORMAN

. . . and the dreaded ape Turkoz
(*TUR-KOZE*)
. . . Squeezed Tarzan in a death grip, his huge fangs seeking out Tarzan's throat. But Tarzan plunged his knife into the ape's breast, again and again, until it rolled lifeless on the ground. Then Tarzan raised his head to the sky and called out the great victory cry of the apes—AHHHHHHH
    (higher) AHHHHHHH.
    (lower) AHHHHHH!!! And Jane Porter fainted dead away.

And Norman drops down, finished. Paul remains transfixed, asking with great interest:

PAUL

Then what'd he do with Jane Porter?

NORMAN *(smiling)*

Continued in next month's *All Story Magazine*.

Paul sinks back, disappointed. A beat, then, lazy:

PAUL

Norm? What're you gonna be when you grow up?

NORMAN

A minister, I guess . . .
    (pause) Or a professional boxer.

PAUL

You think you could beat Jack Johnson?

Norman shrugs.

PAUL

I think you could. I'd lay a bet on it.

NORMAN *(pleased)*

What are you going to be?

PAUL

A professional fly fisherman.

NORMAN

There is no such thing.

PAUL *(sits up, surprised)*

There isn't? Well, then, a professional boxer . . .

NORMAN *(dry)*

Not a minister?

Paul doesn't answer. Both boys stare up at the clouds a moment more, then Paul starts to giggle and Norman follows. They burst into laughter.

18. *EXT. WOODS—DAY. (Still Photo)*

NARRATOR

In 1917, World War I came to Missoula, taking with it every able-bodied lumberjack, leaving the woods to boys and old men. So at sixteen I did my duty and started working for the U.S. Forest Service.

19. *EXT. LOGGING CAMP—DAY. (Still Photo) In a logging camp we find* NORMAN, *full-grown.*

Craig Sheffer as Norman in 1917, during his stint in the Forest Service.

NARRATOR

Paul was too young to join me, and besides, he had decided this early he had two major purposes in life: to fish and not to work, or at least not to allow work to interfere with fishing. In his teens, then, he got a summer job as a lifeguard at the municipal swimming pool, so in the early evenings he could go fishing and during the days he could look over the girls in their bathing suits.

20. EXT. *PUBLIC POOL*—DAY. *(Still Photo)* PAUL, *full-grown, handsome, poses on his lifeguard stand.*

21. EXT. *MOUNTAIN*—DAY. *Norman all alone in his lookout tower.*

22. EXT. *FIELD*—NIGHT. *Paul necks with a girl.*

Brad Pitt as Paul, at his summer job as a lifeguard.

23. INT. THE CHURCH—DAY. The congregation sings "Be Thou My Vision." Paul is now taller than Norman.

NARRATOR

Undoubtedly our differences would not have seemed so great if we had not been such a close family. Painted on one side of our church wall were the words "God is love." We always assumed these three words were spoken directly to the four of us in our family and had no reference outside, which my brother and I soon discovered was full of bastards, the number increasing rapidly the farther one got from Missoula, Montana.

24. EXT. MAIN STREET—DAY. (Still Period Photos) Soldiers march back down Main Street. People cheer. The town has changed.

Paul, Clara, and Norman in church.

NARRATOR

The war ended much as it began, with doughboys marching and the town celebrating their return, everyone believing that this first year of peace would be the best. But no one's 1919 would be better than mine. I considered myself a lumberjack and a poet and, at last, a man, and I intended to make the end of my high school career indelible.

25. INT. *A HOME—NIGHT. A dance. Norman drinks surreptitiously with* CHUB, HUMPH, CONROY, *etc. They all shout with the* SONG *on the* GRAMOPHONE: *"I'll say she does!" Couples dance the "shimmy."*

26. EXT. *RIVER—DAY. Norman and girl sit by river. He reads Wordsworth to her. There are tears in her eyes.*

27. *EXT. COURTHOUSE STEPS—DAY. The gang sits around listening to Norman tell a story about forest fires. They are silent, gripped in his spell.*

NORMAN

. . . then it crested the hill. Did you ever hear a forest fire, coming down on top of you, at sixty miles an hour . . . ?

28. *INT. THE MANSE—DAY. Norman bangs in, runs up the stairs, hearing the Reverend rehearsing in the study. Then:*

REVEREND

Norman.

Norman winces, turns dutifully back.

29. *INT. THE STUDY—DAY. Norman stands in the same spot he stood in as a boy, unable to keep from glancing at the same thorny motto above his father, who sits at his desk tying an elegant fly on a jig, the bright colors glowing in the filtered light.*

REVEREND

I have received a rather disturbing telephone call.

Norman tenses.

REVEREND

From Mrs. Hauser.

NORMAN

Oh . . .

REVEREND

She claims that Paul has . . .
    (delicate) . . . taken advantage of her daughter, Lucy.

[39]

NORMAN

Taken advantage?

REVEREND

Compromised, Norman.
      (sighs, troubled) Actually, the term she used was more . . .
colorful . . .

Norman gapes in sudden comprehension. The Reverend's gaze levels on him, rigorous and demanding.

REVEREND

Is it true?

Norman splutters, honestly amazed, even envious.

NORMAN

What—? *Paul?* My *brother*, Paul?

The Reverend holds his eyes a beat longer, then nods once, willing to accept Norman's denial.

30. *EXT. THE MANSE—NIGHT. A Model T truck, engine cut, rolls silently up as out of an upstairs window the shadowy figure of Paul steps, then leaps wildly off the porch roof and runs to the truck, inside of which is the same gang we've seen before— Humph, Chub, Conroy, etc. Then another figure emerges from the window. It is Norman, who does not jump but lowers himself down the porch post. The* HORN HONKS. *He winces, sprinting to the truck, hissing "Shhh!" as they chant, "PREACHER! PREACHER!" Finally, he hauls himself in, immediately punching everyone.*

31. *INT. THE TRUCK—NIGHT. It rounds a corner and they are all thrown against one side in a heap, laughing and struggling.*

The boys carry the boat toward the chutes.

HUMPH

    Don't spill any—!

He holds up a bottle of hooch and the others grab for it, Norman getting there first, taking a long pull, gasping:

NORMAN

    Moose piss!

Laughter. Conroy, driving, yells back:

CONROY

    Where to?

Everyone speaks together, disagreeing.

EVERYONE

The University! No. Murph's. Again? Toss the pigskin. Oh, thrill. Front Street! (*Etc.*)

31A. EXT. BRIDGE—DAWN. They sit draped around the car, passing the bottle, failed and bored. Then:

NORMAN

Did I tell you what a forest fire sounds like, coming down a . . .

BOYS

Aw, shaddup . . . !

Norman drops back. Another beat, then:

PAUL

I got an idea.

No response.

PAUL

How would you boys like to go down in history?

Now they begin to perk up.

PAUL

We . . . "borrow" old man Seifert's rowboat . . .
   (pauses for effect) . . . and shoot the Chutes?

He gets a blank stare from everyone. Pleased, he takes a drink, waiting. Finally:

EVERYONE

Impossible. Crazy. Stupid. Madman! (*Etc.*)

CONROY

You *can't* shoot the Chutes, Paul.

PAUL

You can try.

HUMPH

You can *die* trying.

PAUL

And they'd bury you with full honors.

His eyes meet Norman's and Norman sees the sheer joy in them and can't resist smiing, both of them grinning now, excited, bursting into laughter. The others, infectei join in, laughing and cursing their fate as the truck drives into the night.

31B. EXT. WOODS—DAWN. Paul, Norman and Chub carry a long wooden rowboi on their heads as the boys stumble through the pitch-black woods, grumbling.

BOYS

This is heaven, Pauly. We passed here already. Which way, O B'wana? (*Etc.*)

CONROY (*tripping*)

Dammit! I don't need a goddam rowboat, I need a womannnn!!

Cheers, laughter. Norman murmurs to Paul:

NORMAN

How about Lucy Hauser?

Paul does a quick doubletake, but says nothing.

Craig Sheffer on the set.

32. EXT. THE CHUTES—DAWN. The old rowboat seems to fly on its own down the slippery embankment.

EVERYONE

AAAAAAAAHHH!!

They manage to stop it just above the void, and, grinning, Paul motions widely. They are standing on a cliff above the highest of a series of waterfalls that snake away into the night. For a moment all they can do is stare, then:

HUMPH

Jesus, Mary and Joseph.

Clearly, they all feel the same way, fear replacing bravado as the liquor wears off. But Paul is still high and excited. He starts to the water.

                                    PAUL

     Come on.

No one moves. Paul imitates a chicken, quietly.

                                    PAUL

     Bawk, bawk, bawk . . .

The others rise as one, angrily, but Paul only smiles.

                                    PAUL

     Alright, alright. Then it's just me, and Norm and Chub.

Chub seems to shrink in size.

                                    CHUB

     Jeez, Pauly . . .

                                    PAUL

     Just me and Norm?

*He looks at Norman who crouches by the bank, expressionless. A look of hurt crosses
Paul's face.*
     But then, Norman smiles jauntily up at him.

                                   NORMAN

     You need ballast, brother.

Paul grins, reaches out and takes Norman's hand firmly, pulling him up.

33. EXT. WATERFALL—DAWN. The first streaks of dawn reflect in the fast-moving river as Chub pushes the boat over the gravel bank and onto the water fifty feet above the Chutes. Spaced along the bank, the boys watch, ashamed, as Paul in the prow and Norman in the stern steer an expert course with their paddles, straight down the gut of the river toward the falls. Unable to let them go, the boys begin to jog next to the boat, running faster as it's caught and pulled along in the current. Paul turns to Norman, smiling, pointing to a splash in the water.

PAUL

Good fishing.

Norman nods, trying to keep his smile intact, unable to stop his chin from shivering. The roar grows louder. Spray envelops Paul. Norman turns one last time to shore, desperate, feeling a scream rise in his throat, and he sees Chub, still running, his expression very worried. Then there is a jolt. Norman snaps back, grabbing both sides, and the prow slides over the falls, poises there for one timeless moment, then plunges.

From above, as the boys stand watching in awed silence, the dark form of the boat whips away, disappearing in a few seconds, only the vague sound of Paul's wild laughter drifting back.

34. EXT. THE TOP—DAWN. The boys strain into the darkness, trying to pick out the boat, but they can see nothing beyond the foam and jagged rocks. They stand a moment, the full impact of what has happened dawning on them. Then, very quiet and frightened:

CHUB

Oh, jeez . . .

35. EXT. THE RIVER—DAWN. Dawn streaks the sky. The boys, soaked, exhausted, scared to death, search up and down the rocky bank, shouting:

[46]

The crew on a raft, during the filming of the chutes scene.

BOYS

Helloooo! Macleans!! Paul-eeee! Preeeeecherrr!!

Then Humph calls to them, his voice quavering. They run up to see the rowboat, bat-
tered and abandoned in a backwater. Cold fear descends on them. For a moment no one
speaks, then Chub breaks off, running away as he yells desperately:

CHUB

MACLAYYYYYNS!!!

And, suddenly, from behind a tree, Paul leaps out.

Shooting the chutes.

PAUL

Bugga bugga bugga!!

Chub jumps as if he's been shot and Paul drops to the ground, dissolving in hysterics as the boys stand there dumbfounded, staring at him. From farther downstream Norman emerges, soaked, an ugly knot on his head, and looks helplessly from the others to Paul, his expression hardening with anger.

36. INT. THE MANSE—MORNING. *The clock ticks. There is no other sound. The Reverend and Mother sit stiffly, unmoving, very worried. Then the truck pulls up outside. Boys' yells, laughs. The truck pulls away. Footsteps approach. The Reverend rises. The boys enter, bedraggled, bruised. Mother stares hard, clamping her jaw against the tears. There is a beat of silence. A chill descends. The boys seem to shrink in size. Then the Reverend speaks, his voice cold and controlled.*

Chub (Michael Cuditz) falls backward as Paul jumps out from behind a tree.

REVEREND

You will go to church today and pray for forgiveness.

The boys murmur assent.

REVEREND

Your mother spent the night sick with worry. Did you give any thought to *her* feelings?

Pained, Norman hangs his head.

REVEREND

Who gave you the boat?

NORMAN

We . . .

Brad Pitt on the set.

PAUL *(very quiet)*

We borrowed it . . .

REVEREND

Borrowed? What have you *done*?

He drills Norman with his eyes.

REVEREND

You will work off every cent of its value.

NORMAN

Yes, sir.

Paul and Norman fight.

PAUL

I'll work it off, Father. It was my idea.

Taken completely by surprise, the Reverend allows his expression free rein for a beat, and Norman can't miss the flash of pride in it.

37. INT. KITCHEN—LATER. Paul walks in as Norman is making himself a sandwich. Mugging, he raises his eyebrows and wipes his forehead, breathing a big "Wooooh . . . !" as in "Did we get caught or what?" He laughs, sharing the moment with Norman, unaware that Norman is not at all amused. Then he spots Norman's sandwich and shakes his head.

PAUL

What's *that*? No, here's what you want, brother. Ham, cheese, sardines . . .

NORMAN *(an edge of warning)*

I hate sardines.

Paying no attention, Paul takes over Norman's sandwich.

PAUL

Let me. Boy, did you hear 'em? They're going to tell everybody
that the class of '19 did it. You know what? I should write an ar-
ticle—"Macleans Conquer Chutes!"
   (puts sardines on)

That'd shut 'em up. You could get it in the school paper . . .

NORMAN

I don't want sardines.

PAUL *(shakes head)*

Class of '19 my hind end. I can still see Chub with that . . . sheep
face of his . . . "Jeez Pauly."

NORMAN *(harder)*

I don't *want* sardines, Paul . . .

PAUL *(laughs, piling more on Norman's sandwich)*

What a Skeezix . . .

NORMAN *(his voice hard)*

I don't want god*damn* sardines . . .

*And out of nowhere, Norman swings his right arm as hard as he can, catching Paul
on the ear, knocking him backward into the table, the sandwich flying off.*

PAUL

He-e-ey . . . !

Without grace or elegance, Norman wades in, his eyes flat with rage, a strange fright-
ening sound rising from him.

PAUL

Hey . . . what the *hell*?!

And he rises to his full height, towering over Norman, and responds, bellowing, flail-
ing, both of them swinging as hard as they can in a flurry of madness. They don't feel
the blows that rain on their faces, blood spattering their clothes. And then Mother is
there, horrified, running toward them, arms out, pushing in between.

MOTHER

Stop! Stop! Stop!!

But they pay no attention to her, trying to fight through her. Only her hair shows be-
tween them, bobbing up and down, and then suddenly it's gone as she slips on the fallen
food, and drops heavily onto the floor, her glasses skittering away. Both boys stop in-
stantly, staring in shock. Then they yell:

NORMAN AND PAUL

You *hit* her! You son of a bitch! You knocked my mother down!
(Etc.)

They launch themselves like madmen, and the fight resumes, even wilder than before,
as Mother scrabbles, pulling herself up between them, chicken salad and sardines cling-
ing to her dress.

MOTHER

No! I slipped, I just slipped . . .

And she staggers around in circles, groping blindly at both boys as they fight on, mur-
muring, crying:

[53]

MOTHER

Stop. Please. I slipped, that's all. Please. I just *slipped* . . .

NARRATOR

That was the only time we ever fought. Perhaps we wondered afterward which of us was tougher, but, if boyhood questions aren't answered before a certain point, they can't be raised again. So we returned to being gracious to one another, as the church wall suggested.

38. EXT. THE BIG BLACKFOOT RIVER—DAY. The Reverend, Paul and Norman cast, their lines catching the light, their flies hitting the water. Norman casts just like his father, precise, conservative. Paul has a stronger, more daring, even flamboyant style.

Suddenly, the black head of a huge trout breaks the surface, snapping up a fly.

In the shallows, Paul feels the pull and strikes. The Reverend notices with appreciation Paul's strength and style. Norman struggles briefly with his catch, then pulls it out of the water, proudly.

Paul moves with his fish to the bank, delighted.

PAUL

A monster . . . !

REVEREND

Beautiful.

Norman and Paul lay their fish side by side on the bank, both boys tensing slightly with the competition. Sensing this, the Reverend says, sincerely:

REVEREND

They are both marvels.

And he drops his creel in front of them, pulling out a behemoth trout. Laid next to the boys', it is clearly the winner. The boys laugh in acknowledgment, the tension dissolving. The Reverend is careful to add:

[54]

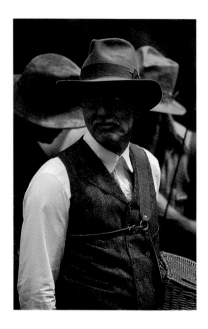

Tom Skerritt on the set.

REVEREND

I'd say the Lord has blessed us all today.

But, as he puts the fish back, he can't resist:

REVEREND

It's just that he's been *particularly* gracious to me.

And he starts off, grinning happily.

39. EXT. TRAIN STATION—DAY. *Norman is dressed in a suit and high collar. Luggage is piled next to him. The rest of the family stand stiffly, none of them liking farewells.*

The reverend and Clara see Norman off to Dartmouth.

NARRATOR

The year ended with my acceptance into Dartmouth College. Some time before, Father had taken me aside and told me that I could go to any college in the world that would admit me. I knew he earned no more than 1800 dollars a year, so his offer meant more to me than anything in my life. And, in the autumn of 1919, I boarded the Northern Pacific for a three-thousand-mile trip east, to the unknown.

Boarding begins. Norman holds out his hand for a formal farewell from the Reverend, then to Mother who resists the urge to hug him. Instead, she gives him the barest peck on the cheek. Finally, he turns to Paul, who beams, proud of his older brother, and shakes his hand with love. Then Norman hurries aboard and the train huffs out of the station, Norman looking back at the last moment, already homesick, but the family is lost in great puffs of steam.

Norman at Dartmouth.

NARRATOR

And, though I came back to Montana in the summers, between the Forest Service and college I was away from home nearly all of the next several years.

40. EXT. COLLEGE—DAY. (Still Period Photo Montage) An ivy-covered Eastern college, brick buildings, football games, men in raccoon coats, etc.

Paul graduates from the University of Montana.

NARRATOR

During that time, my father was elected Presbyterian Council President of the entire Intermountain West, an honor Mother felt even more strongly than he did. Paul decided to stay home for college, unwilling to leave the great rivers of Montana, and the fish he hadn't yet caught. When he was done with college, he took a job as a reporter for the *Helena Bee* and moved to that town, his connection with the family dwindling, growing almost as sparse as my own.

41. *EXT./INT. MONTAGE OF PAUL—DAY. Stills of the family, church, Paul in college, Paul fishing, Paul with his diploma, Paul as a reporter, the* Helena Bee *office, etc.*

Paul at the Helena Bee.

42. EXT. COLLEGE—DAY. Still of Norman with a diploma stands wearing mortar-board and gown.

NARRATOR

As a part of my degree, I was required to enlighten incoming freshmen on the wonders of the Romantic poets.

43. EXT. COLLEGE—DAY. An ivy-covered college hall.

44. INT. A CLASSROOM—DAY. Norman recites Wordsworth. He is mature and well dressed, his manner and delivery just like the Reverend's.

NARRATOR

And, although I was unaware of it at the time, teaching fit me.

Norman teaches at Dartmouth, 1925.

45. *INT. FRAT HOUSE—NIGHT. Norman plays poker with frat brothers, a cigarette dangling from his lips, his expression shrewd and tough.*

NARRATOR

But most of those years I spent in the card room of my fraternity house, giving my blue-nosed brothers a lesson in Front Street poker. Unfortunately, despite these years of education, I lacked the one thing that was most important, a vocation. Neither poker nor even Wordsworth had provided me a clear direction, and I returned uncertain of my future, and ashamed of my uncertainty.

46. *EXT. THE WEST—DAY. A train clacks past the spectacular Rockies.*

47. *INT. THE TRAIN—DAY. Norman sits looking out the window as the Big Blackfoot River comes* INTO VIEW. *He smiles, relieved.*

48. EXT. THE STATION—DAY. Norman descends with his luggage and sees his parents approach through the crowd. They are grayer and older, and to them Norman seems a miraculously full-grown, cosmopolitan man. As formal as ever, the Reverend shakes Norman's hand. Mother smiles warmly, and pecks his cheek in the same spot.

49. INT. THE MANSE—DAY.

> MOTHER

Dinner is in half an hour, you have time for a bath. The towels are on your bed. I put out one of your father's robes. Do you have any decent socks? Take a pair of Father's if you don't. Not his argyles. We're having a ham . . .

She winds down, allowing herself to study her son in the privacy of their home. Norman smiles at her concern.

> NORMAN

Do I look thin, Mother?

She smiles back, then asks shyly:

> MOTHER

Do I look old, Norman?

Norman is completely surprised by this uncharacteristic question. He reacts vehemently.

> NORMAN

No, Mother. You . . .
> (searching) You look . . .

MOTHER *(quickly saving him)*

I wish Paul could have been here tonight. He's working late . . .

And she hurries into the kitchen. Alone, he looks around the quiet, unchanged house a moment. Everything seems smaller, older, familiar, strange. He catches sight of himself in the hall tree mirror, an adult in a fashionable suit, his face thinner, more mature. He leans closer in the dim light and smiles, not displeased, then starts up the staircase two at a time, and his FATHER'S VOICE *calls, exactly as it used to.*

REVEREND

Norman?

And Norman is a child again, caught.

REVEREND

Would you come in, please?

Dutifully, he turns back and trudges down the hall.

50. INT. FATHER'S STUDY—DAY. *Norman's eyes go immediately to the plaque.* "No One Will Touch Me With Impunity." *He stops before the polished desk in the same place he always has, but the Reverend motions him to the oversized red leather armchair.*

REVEREND

I'm sorry Paul won't be here.
    (shrugs, smiling) The life of a newspaperman . . . And now he seems to have taken on the whole of Anaconda mining. You know how he likes to . . .
    (makes a blade of his hand)

Norman arrives home from college.

NORMAN *(smiles)*

I do.

Then the Reverend's face clouds with concern.

REVEREND

I also hear that he . . .

But he changes his mind, blinking, smiling abruptly, Norman noticing the change.

REVEREND

Well. I hear everything, don't I? Lord forbid any of my flock leave me in ignorance.

Norman laughs.

REVEREND

Yes, and *you* can expect that everyone from here to Helena knows the details of your education.

Norman smiles, pleased and embarrassed, as the Reverend passes his judgment with sincerity:

REVEREND

It is an achievement, Norman.

And Norman basks in the rarely spoken approval.

REVEREND

And, so, to what use shall you put that achievement?

NORMAN *(caught)*

I'm . . . not sure.

The Reverend keeps staring at him. Norman casts around.

NORMAN

Uhh, well . . . I was, um, considering the Forest Service . . .

REVEREND *(shocked)*

As a *career*?

NORMAN *(quickly)*

No, no. For the summer . . .

REVEREND *(great relief)*

Ah. A break. A good idea. The body fuels the mind . . .

NORMAN *(relieved)*

Yes, that's . . .

REVEREND

And after?

NORMAN

After? I'm . . . I'm not absolutely . . .
  (struggles) . . . sure.

REVEREND *(anger rising)*

But you've had *six* years to *become* sure, Norman . . .

Controlling himself, he reaches unconsciously for a red pencil from the same old mug.
Norman sighs.

REVEREND

All right, well . . .
  (taps pencil) . . . have you considered an advanced degree, then?
The law . . . ?

NORMAN

No.

REVEREND

Medicine?

NORMAN

No.

REVEREND

The ministry?

NORMAN *(quickly)*

I've applied for several teaching positions . . .

REVEREND *(brightens)*

You have?

NORMAN

Yes. College level. I haven't heard . . .

REVEREND *(clearly pleased)*

No, it's early. But . . . well, you've taught classes already, haven't you?

Norman nods.

REVEREND

And you feel the experience was rewarding? I mean to say, you feel that this could be your . . .
  (hopeful) . . . calling?

NORMAN *(struggling)*

Calling . . . ?

He can't look up at the Reverend's disappointment. Then Mother interrupts, calling happily:

MOTHER *(v.o.)*

Dinner! Gentlemen . . . !

51. *INT. THE* HELENA BEE—. *Norman walks into the foyer. People are hurrying back and forth, busy, intense. He hears laughter and looks into an office full of men in their shirtsleeves, smoking cigars and drinking, all talking at once. Among them is Paul, an adult now, golden, easy, assured. Norman just studies him a moment in silence, amazed that his little brother has grown up.*

PAUL

If it's so funny, how come I'm not laughing . . . ?

MAN #1

Pee in their pants?

HARRY

Pee in their *pants*?

PAUL

Pee in their pants, yes. The rules at Anaconda say no breaks, not even for the john, so the poor bastards have to stand there and pee in their pants . . .

HARRY

Well, that's not a bad story, but I got a better one . . .

MAN #1 *(echoing Paul)*

Pee in their pants . . .

HARRY

I got a better one—what about the late . . . ?

MAN #2

George Masterson.

[67]

MAN #1

His *widow* . . .

PAUL

I'll take that story. *(laughs)*

MAN #2

She's twenty-three, and built like a brick . . .

PAUL

It'll be a hardship, but . . .

MAN #1

Twenty-*two* . . .

HARRY

No, I'll take it. You take the Anaconda thing, and I'll . . .

PAUL

Oh, no, I'm the reporter, Harry, I'll interview the grieving widow . . .

HARRY

But I'm the boss, Maclean . . .

PAUL *(laughs)*

Fine by me, Boss. But if you do go see her, make sure you button your fly first.

Harry looks down. His fly is wide open. As everyone laughs, Paul sees Norman. Surprised, he stares a beat, then lights up, both men smiling at each other with pure happiness.

PAUL

Brother . . . !

He strides toward Norman as if he's going to hug him, only at the last moment pulling back and shaking his hand firmly instead, both men looking slightly away. Then Paul announces proudly:

PAUL

This is my big brother, boys—the pro*fessor.*

The men wave, greet Norman as Paul leads him away.

NORMAN

Thanks for coming to see me last night.

PAUL

Damn, I'm sorry I couldn't make it. I wanted to be there. I wanted to hear the old man say . . .
  (perfect imitation) Norman, would you come into the study, please?

Norman laughs ruefully. Paul looks away.

PAUL

How do they . . . look to you?

NORMAN

Older . . .

Paul nods. Neither looks at the other. Then Paul squeezes Norman's arm, speaking quietly, with real admiration.

PAUL

Jeez. The professor.
(Norman colors, Paul turns breezy) We should celebrate . . .

NORMAN

I'm back.

He leads Norman to a corner and pulls out a brown-bagged bottle. Norman glances at the clock overhead, reading 10:35.

NORMAN

Little early for me.

PAUL

The East is making you soft, brother . . .

and Norman grabs the bottle and gulps it, gasping at the vile hooch. Paul laughs, delighted. Then:

PAUL

Hey. Did you do much fishing out East?

NORMAN *(sadly)*

None.

PAUL

Well, then, what say?
(loud) The hell with Anaconda. How about the Big Blackfoot instead?

And Norman laughs like a boy, happy and excited.

52. EXT. ROAD—DAY. Paul's car drives past heady views to the river.

Craig Sheffer and Brad Pitt.

53. EXT. THE BIG BLACKFOOT—DAY. Norman follows Paul down the bank to the beautiful, familiar river. For a moment he stops, cocking his head, listening hard. All the subtle SOUNDS *of the* RIVER *sweep over him, the "words" that he's listened to all his life. Goosebumps rise on his skin.*

PAUL *(v.o.)*

Set?

Norman drags himself back from the moment.

NORMAN

Hold on . . .

And he picks up the rod, holding it out, watching the tip beat with his pulse. He can't help chuckling with pleasure. Paul smiles at him, then turns and starts upstream. Norman follows.

Norman lands a fish.

54. *EXT. BIG BLACKFOOT/HOLE—DAY. Norman stops at the first "hole," a back-wash of dirty foam and insects out a way in the water. Trees and brush crowd the shore-line so that he can't try an overhead cast for fear of tangling his line in the branches behind him.*

He's forced to attempt a "roll" cast, one that doesn't move the rod rearward at all. It is difficult and Norman can't help glancing upstream at Paul, who has settled at the next hole trying very hard not to watch. Norman's first cast is shaky. He tries again, a small improvement. Paul watches openly now, unable to turn away, and finally speaks, gently:

PAUL

The fish are out farther.

Norman doesn't react, doesn't turn. He reels his line in slowly, his back to Paul, who adds quickly, shrugging:

PAUL

Just a little farther . . .

He hesitates, trying to turn away, sensing Norman tense. A long beat, then, sweetly, wanting to help:

PAUL

Cast your line *into* the current, that'll give you a better base, add some distance . . .

Neither man looks at the other. Norman acts as if he hasn't heard anything at all, and Paul turns away immediately and marches out of sight around the bend. But the moment he's gone, Norman follows his directions precisely, casting ten feet farther, right into the edge of the hole. He looks quickly around, but Paul is gone, and he allows himself to smile at his newfound ability. Again, he casts, putting solid power into the fragile rod. The line sails out and lands light as a feather right in the center of the backwash. Almost instantly, the fly disappears and Norman knows he has hooked a big one. Setting the hook, he strides into the fast current unheeding, concentrating everything on the play of the line, the fish fighting but inexorably losing ground until, exhausted, it surfaces, a long, dark form in the swirling backwash. Norman lands it on a sandbar. He stands looking down at the beautiful, iridescent trout.

55. EXT. THE RIVER—DAY. A changed man, Norman walks along the bank, smiling proudly, hoping to run into Paul with his bulging basket weighing on his shoulder, the trout's tail sticking out the back, proclaiming its magnificent size.

But as he rounds the bend, he is struck by a sight that brings him to a halt.

Paul has managed to climb a chunk of cliff in the middle of the river and Norman watches him standing at the top in the clearest blue sky, beginning to "reverse cast," an intricate and dramatic process used to tempt the fish below. First he casts hard upstream, skimming the water with his fly, but never letting it touch. Then he pivots, reversing his line in a great oval above his head and driving it low and hard downstream, again skimming the water with his fly. This he repeats over and over, his wet shirt open, revealing the play of his muscles, rainbows forming in the vapor around him.

Norman is awed, humbled, overwhelmed by his beauty, by the perfection of his movement. Then he hears VOICES *behind him and turns, annoyed, as if they are vi-*

Paul casts.

olating something sacred. It is a MIDDLE-AGED COUPLE, *both carrying fishing rods, the woman wearing big overalls and big boots, and they too are caught by the scene, staring in astonishment. The woman sits, smoothing the pine needles without looking, murmuring:*

WOMAN

My, my.

And her husband breathes in response:

HUSBAND

Jesus.
    (a beat; then again) Jesus.

And Norman feels himself begin to smile with pride as Paul stands unaware, alone, suspended in his perfect place. Then Norman turns and walks away.

WOMAN

Wait . . . Don't you want to see what he catches?

NORMAN *(over his shoulder)*

I don't have to. He's my brother . . .

And he walks off, smiling.

56. EXT. COURTHOUSE STEPS—NIGHT. The old gang sit in their familiar places, listening, as in the old days, to Norman telling a story.
    On their faces are soft, reminiscent smiles, everyone loving this return to their past.

NORMAN

In my . . . sophomore year, I decided to join the boxing team.
And one day my coach said to me, "Mac, how'd you like to meet
John L. Sullivan." *John L. Sullivan*! Can you imagine? The last
bare-knuckle champion of the world!

He stands, posing in the old-fashioned straight-back style, fists high in front of him.

NORMAN

So, we went down to Boston, to this little—shack, and we walk
inside and there stands my hero—dressed in a Union suit with his
gut hanging down to his knees. "John," says Coach, "I'd like you
to meet a boxer of mine—Mac Maclean." And Sullivan says to
me, "Is that *Mc*lean or *Mac*lean? Irish or Scot?" And I say, "Scot.
Sir."
    (chuckles) He smiles at me as friendly as can be, and he says,
"The Scots, a *filthy* people."

*Norman mugs his own amazed response. Chuckles, murmurs from the boys. Norman
is up and acting now, doing John L. with a brogue.*

NORMAN

Then he says, "Do you know how they come by the Highland
Jig? Well, it seems they live in these here sod huts up in the High-
lands, and it gets ferocious cold up there in the wintertime. So
when nature calls, they run to the outhouse, but the cold prevents
'em from makin' it all the way, and they squat right there and do
it on the ground."

Everyone laughs in disbelief.

NORMAN

"Well, by the time spring rolls around, there are piles of human
excrement all the way out to the trench. And you know what
they have to do then? They have to jump between them *piles*!"
And then this huge, fat, old man puts his hands up over his head
like a ballerina, and does the goddamn Highland Jig for me . . . !

*Norman demonstrates, springing, twirling, singing a jig, the others laughing in
amazement. Finally, he drops down, shaking his head at the mortifying memory.*

NORMAN

Which just goes to show, that the world is full of *bastards*, the . . .

Grinning, knowing, Paul joins in perfect sync.

NORMAN AND PAUL

. . . number increasing rapidly, the farther one gets from Missoula, Montana.

The brothers smile warmly at each other. The others applaud, joking and laughing.

HUMPH

See? That's why you have to stick around here from now on.

General agreement.

CONROY

Hey, where's the gargle? Didn't you visit uncle?

RILEY *(handing flask around)*

Never fear . . .

CHUB *(to Norman)*

Say, I got it. I'm gonna take you to the Fourth of July dance. Every girl you need to know will be there. With*out* mama. We'll find you a Sheba . . .

Big laughs at the term. The courthouse BELL SOUNDS *the hour.*

CHUB

She'll keep you here. C'mon, what do you say, and don't say no.

Before Norman can answer, Paul rises.

PAUL

Well, gentlemen, it's been swell, but I must rush . . .

Warmly and almost surreptitiously, he squeezes Norman's shoulder as he walks to his car. The others smirk and nod knowingly.

CONROY

Heavy date, Paul?

HUMPH *(snorts)*

With a poker table.
(*chuckles*)

[77]

CHUB

Hey, you see they got new signs on the road down, Pauly? "Does your husband misbehave? Grunt and grumble, rant and rave? Shoot the brute some . . .

EVERYONE

. . . Burma-Shave!"

Big laughs as Paul gets into his car, waving breezily back. Norman asks Chub:

NORMAN

The road down to where?

CHUB *(waggling his eyebrows)*

Lolo.

Norman looks at Paul, who honks the AOOGAH HORN *and drives off, as the Narrator begins speaking:*

NARRATOR

Lolo Hot Springs was a few miles outside of Missoula, at the end of a dark canyon.

57. EXT. LOLO—NIGHT. Paul's car sits beneath a faded ornate sign reading "LOLO HOT SPRINGS—THE SPRINGS ETERNAL SALVE FOR A WORRIED WORLD." Beyond it is a ramshackle resort building. From its windows comes the only light at the end of a long, dark road.

Paul.

NARRATOR

Originally, it was a resort for the wealthy, who came to take its healing waters. But by the mid-twenties it had become a gambling joint, and the only water taken was by whores who came to boil out in the springs.

Next to the building lies abandoned a pool of bubbling water, steam from it rising into the night.

NARRATOR

Unlike the saloons along Front Street, there was a silence at Lolo. And it was lethal. Men came for one reason—to play poker. They didn't play it well, either. The only thing you could know about a Lolo player, was that he hated to lose . . .

58. EXT. THE CHURCH—DAY. *From inside, the* REVEREND'S VOICE *can be heard, preaching.*

59. INT. THE CHURCH—DAY. *The Macleans still sit in the first pew, making Paul's absence apparent. Norman studies the Reverend, smiling slightly, appreciating his ability.*

NARRATOR

Being back in my father's church seemed to complete my return. The same faces gazed up at him. The same sign stood above us all. But it was my father's words that made me feel most at home.

REVEREND

. . . I have a very poor opinion of the man or woman who fails to find pleasure in the memories of youth. It would be sad to think that they were all forgotten, and furnished pleasure no more, and that there was no sweet wistfulness for the touch of a vanished hand and the sound of a voice that is still. And in the glow of awakened memories, with the tenderest feelings of the heart all astir, we are reminded of the poet who sings—"Backward, turn backward, O time in your flight. Make me a child again just for tonight . . ."

The Reverend's words roll out, soft and poetic and moving; the congregation is silent, caught in the beauty of the sermon. On the wall is the sign which still proclaims "God is Love."

60. EXT. PAVILION—DUSK—ESTABLISHING SHOT.

61. EXT. PAVILION—NIGHT. *A banner hanging from the ceiling proclaims:*

FOURTH OF JULY
DANCE AND FIREWORKS

A LIVE BAND *including a female saxophonist plays behind a crooner while couples fox-trot in a tight knot. Into this madhouse walk Norman and Chub, who wears baggy bell-bottoms, saddle shoes and a striped blazer. He rubs his hands together and grins widely.*

                              CHUB

Recognize anybody?

                            NORMAN

Um . . .

                              CHUB

You've been gone too long, son. Ohh, *look* it . . .

                            NORMAN

Where?

                              CHUB

Mary Norton.
        (chortles) Calls herself Mar*ie* now.

                            NORMAN

Where . . . ?

Then Norman recognizes the big, healthy-looking girl. But as she turns a smaller girl comes INTO VIEW, *wearing a man's snap-brim hat set rakishly on her head. Norman is jolted. There is an essence that emanates from her, a glow. She is laughing, with an edge of danger, as Chub goes on:*

                              CHUB

Thinks she's Joan Crawford since . . .

NORMAN *(interrupts)*

Who's the . . .
   (she's blocked) . . . with the hat . . . ?

CHUB

Where?

Norman pulls him halfway onto the dance floor until she comes INTO VIEW *again.*

NORMAN

Her.

CHUB

Oh. Ohh, yeah.
   (smiles) In-fatuated?

NORMAN

(colors)

Chub . . .

CHUB *(grins at his discomfort)*

Jessie Burns, from Wolf Creek. Her brother went to Hollywood.

NORMAN

Jessie Burns . . .

As he speaks the musicians strike up "Runnin' Wild" and JESSIE *is swept onto the dance floor by a handsome young man. The two do a fast fox-trot, Jessie's short skirt flaring around her slim legs, showing her rolled stockings. Norman stares hotly.*

CHUB

Swishhh.

He sighs, takes a swig from his flask, and holds it out to Norman, but Norman isn't there, and Chub keeps turning in a full circle, puzzled.

62. *INT. OTHER SIDE OF PAVILION—NIGHT. The song ends. The dancers applaud. The young man releases Jessie and Norman pops up before her, trying to be suave.*

NORMAN

Dance?

She turns to him, dizzied from the last spin, but before she can respond, the BAND *begins "Bye Bye Blackbird." Immediately open and friendly, she smiles, fanning her face, and leans close so he can hear.*

JESSIE

Would you be a darb and get us a drink?

NORMAN *(can refuse her nothing)*

Sure.

He tries to saunter casually to the punchbowl. As he fills the cups, he turns to her with a prepared, jaunty smile, but she isn't looking. She's pulling her stockings up her thighs, rerolling them. His breath catches. Two other girls come up, panting and red-faced, full of talk, and Norman finds himself hurrying back, walking like Groucho Marx so as not to spill the drinks. Jessie steps away from the girls to meet him.

JESSIE

A lifesaver . . . !

She gulps down the drink. A little dribbles on her chin. She wipes at it with her hand.

[83]

JESSIE

How ladylike.

Norman laughs, charmed by her forthrightness.

NORMAN

Just a sec . . .

He pats his pockets, pulls out a clean white handkerchief, then, surprising her, he dabs gently at her face.

JESSIE

Oh.
　　(*smiles*) Have to be careful. You'll wipe off all the powder. Phantom of the Opera.

They both laugh. Then there is a pause. Neither knows what to say. Jessie sings along with the band.

JESSIE

Bye, Bye, Blackbird . . .

Feeling it all slipping away, he plunges:

NORMAN

You know, I . . . I heard this song in a little speak in . . . Greenwich Village. New York. And, um, you know who was singing it? Louie Armstrong.

JESSIE

Really?

NORMAN *(relaxing, getting suave)*

Yes. Yeah, this little place we used to go down to every once in a while, best jazz in the world. Colored jazz, y'know? The real McCoy. Not Paul Whiteman, or . . .
  (snorts) . . . the Clicquot Club Eskimos.

JESSIE *(her smile thinning)*

My mother loves the Clicquot Club Eskimos.

NORMAN *(smirk failing)*

Does she?

Desperate, Norman gives up all pretense, and turns to her, open and hopeful.

NORMAN

Dance?

Silently, she raises her slender right arm into the dance position and he places his hand against hers, the contact electric, and at that moment a VOICE *yells through the megaphone cutting the* BAND *off:*

MAN ON STAGE

Yowsah, yowsah, yowsah—let the fireworks beegin!

A rocket lights up the sky. Everyone hurries toward the river. The two girls appear and sweep Jessie away with them, leaving Norman looking into emptiness as the FIREWORKS EXPLODE *above him.*

63. INT. THE MANSE—DAY. Norman paces the house, through the silent living room, past the study in which the Reverend works, down the hall to the kitchen where Mother stands talking into the wooden wall phone.

Jessie Burns (Emily Lloyd).

MOTHER

. . . organizing a relief effort for the poor souls out there, so I'm calling every able body in the congregation . . .

(listens) Me, too, Eva. The worst day of the week. So, I've just pushed things off because we feel—Doctor Maclean and I—that this is so important . . .

(pause) I have a wonderful idea—what better lesson for those girls than a trip to the reservation?

(ignores what may be a protest) To learn a real Christian lesson in giving . . .

(oblivious) Don't you think?

(satisfied) I'll organize it. Don't lift a finger. And thank you, Eva. This is the most charitable idea I've heard in years.

She hangs up, noticing Norman, and goes right on.

MOTHER

Do you know that the children out there don't even have shoes.
Norman . . . ? Oh, were you waiting for the phone?

NORMAN

No, if you're busy . . .

MOTHER

No. Go ahead . . .

NORMAN

No . . .

MOTHER

No, I need a rest.

And she walks off, trying not to smile at him as he calls weakly after her:

NORMAN

No, it's . . . I don't have to . . .

He waits until she is gone, then pulls the door closed and, sighing, picks up the receiver.

NORMAN

Hello, Mrs. Hatcher, I'd . . .
    (pause) Fine. They're all . . . everybody's fine. Um, I'd like the
Burns' residence in Wolf Creek, please.
    (closes eyes) Yes, I know it's a long distance, Mrs. Hatcher.
Thank you.

The phone rings.

Hello. Is Jessie there? This is . . . Well, Norman Maclean, but I don't think she . . .

(waits, then hearing Jessie's voice, he melts) Hello.

(pause) Uh, no, I'm the one who brought you a drink . . .

No, we didn't get a chance. The fireworks started and, and . . . um, we talked about the music?

(nothing) And I said . . .

(hates himself) I heard Louie Armstrong sing the . . .

(winces) Yeah. Me.

I . . . I was a little nervous, it just . . .

Huh? Well, because you're so . . . uhhh . . .

He can't say the word beautiful, so he grins mischievously and does an overripe French accent.

Je ne sais quoi.

(laughs) Yeah, so, anyway, I called because I thought maybe I could come over and listen to the Clicquot Club Eskimos with your mother . . .

(He lights up.) No, but I really would like to see you, that's why I . . .

What? Um, well . . . Saturday?

Well, this Saturday, or . . .

Uhh . . . eight?

Okay. *Okay.* That's just . . .

Right, I'll see you then. I'll . . .

Bye.

(He hangs up, dumbfounded, then breaks into a grin.)

The sheik strikes again.

Jessie and Norman greet Paul and Mabel outside of the speakeasy.

64. *EXT. FRONT STREET—NIGHT. The Reverend's Model T turns down Front Street and parks along the crowded sidewalk. Norman hops out, his hair plastered, wearing a summer suit and outrageous bow tie. He opens the door for Jessie, who takes his hand and steps down, smiling at him with Clara Bow lips, her hair a wavy bob, her dress shimmery and short. They turn up an alley and Norman is about to knock on a hidden door, when:*

PAUL *(v.o.)*

There they are . . .

They turn to see Paul, all dressed in white, smiling happily, walking arm-in-arm with a stunning Indian woman, her straight black hair long, her dress daringly low-cut. Immediately, Norman tenses with worry, shooting a glance at Jessie, but her eyes stay on Paul as they approach. With a tinge of jealousy, he murmurs drily:

NORMAN

Jessie, this is my baby brother, Paul.

Paul laughs, shakes her hand firmly, looking straight at her.

NORMAN

And this is . . . this is Moh-Na-Se-Tah.

With a slightly tough edge she corrects him.

MABEL

Mabel.

Paul saves the moment effortlessly, rapping at the door. A panel opens, revealing the Doorman, who recognizes Paul and swings the door wide, the noise and smoke from the speakeasy inside pouring out.

65. *INT. SPEAKEASY—NIGHT.* MURPHY, *older, but still powerful, comes forward as they enter.*

MURPHY

Hey, Pauly.

PAUL

Murph.

Then he sees Norman and lights up.

MURPHY

Preacher!

JESSIE *(puzzled, to Norman)*

Preacher?

Emily Lloyd between takes.

MURPHY *(shaking Norman's hand, as he leads them in)*

Long time, long time . . .

Then he catches Mabel out of the corner of an eye and his smile vanishes.
He throws out a meaty arm, blocking Paul and Mabel from entering.

MURPHY

You know the house rules as good as I do, Paul—no *Injuns*,
period.

Norman stiffens. Jessie scowls. Mabel looks like a warrior of old, but Paul keeps smil-
ing, only his eyes turning dangerous.

PAUL

Yeah, but the trouble is, Murph, I just flat don't like the house
rules. Period.

MABEL

Me neither.

MURPHY *(tensing)*

What're you gonna make me do here, Pauly?

PAUL

Just get us a table, that's all. For *four*.

They look at each other for a long moment, Paul's expression smiling but unrelenting. Norman sees Jessie's anger, fear, even excitement. He takes a step forward to help, but Murphy drops his arm, saying meaningfully:

MURPHY

Last time, Paul.

And Paul breezes past, leading Mabel. He sees Norman's tense discomfort and just heads down the stairway, smiling.

PAUL

C'mon. You can get back at him by drinking too much and taking all your clothes off . . .

Jessie laughs, surprised. Then Mabel adds, deadly serious:

MABEL

And beat hell out of the sonofabitch.

Norman winces. They walk down the stairs, noticing the disapproving faces looking up. Oblivious, Paul snags a passing waitress.

PAUL

Molly, my darling . . .
   (to others) C'mon. They got swell hooch here. They even wash
the glasses.

Jessie chuckles. They find a table.

PAUL

What'll it be? They have some liqueurs they smuggled in, sweet
and not too . . .

JESSIE

I'll have a martini.

PAUL *(impressed)*

Well. Rightyo. And . . .
   (observes Norman's stiffness) I guess the regular for Norman
here—gin and prune juice?

*This cracks everyone up, even Norman, who relents, giving in to his brother's
jolliness.*

NORMAN

Please, a double.

MABEL *(still angry)*

I want a double, too. Whiskey.

*Paul and Norman glance at each other. An awkward beat, then Norman tries to make
conversation.*

NORMAN

So . . . where are you working now, Mabel?

MABEL *(challenging)*

I sell bait.

Norman tightens, but Jessie just smiles and turns to Mabel, saying, in that innocent and sincere way of hers:

JESSIE

You have the most beautiful hair I've ever seen.

Taken completely by surprise Mabel can only touch her hair self-consciously.

MABEL

Do you think I should get it bobbed?

JESSIE

Not in a million years.

And Mabel smiles for the first time, her toughness dissolving. Proud of Jessie, Norman gives Paul a look of triumph and Paul raises his glass in concession.

PAUL

Well . . .

But before he can think of a toast:

NORMAN

My candle burns at both ends.
It will not last the night.
But ah my foes and oh my friends
It gives a lovely light.

His reading is simple, but touches the others, raising goosebumps on Jessie's bare arms. Mabel looks at him with new eyes, and murmurs, half-embarrassed:

MABEL

. . . That's nice . . .

Cut to THE BAND.

They play a bluesy tune. The waitress, MOLLY, *carries a tray of drinks to:*

Cut to THE TABLE.

Before Norman can raise his glass, Paul makes the toast.

PAUL

Well, how about—to my editor, the old far . . . the old "curmud-
geon" . . .
  (laughter) . . . who just took me off the Anaconda story . . .
  (to Jessie) I'm a reporter at the *Bee.*

JESSIE

I know.

NORMAN *(surprised)*

How do you know?

PAUL *(trying not to gloat)*

I'm famous.

JESSIE

"The Fishing Newspaperman."

NORMAN

You know he *fishes*, too?

MABEL *(dry)*

Everybody knows he fishes.

PAUL

You've been away a long time, brother. Anyway, the old . . . my editor has been getting calls. No names, just threats.

Norman sees Jessie bite the hook.

JESSIE

Real threats?

PAUL

It's nice to know you're touching a nerve, but . . .

JESSIE

What'd they say?

PAUL *(shrugs)*

Oh . . .

NORMAN

You'll have to cut it out of him.

PAUL *(smiles)*

The usual . . .
   (imitates gangster) Some'a the boys are gonna come down and pay me a little visit . . .

Laughter. Then, surprisingly, Jessie does her own impression.

JESSIE

Fit you wit a pair 'a concrete galoshes . . .

Startled, Paul laughs out loud. Norman can't miss the clear attraction between them.

Paul and Mabel (Nicole Burdette) dance.

SONG

My memories cling to me by moonlight on Honolu-lu Bay.
And all the beaches are filled with peaches
Who bring their ukes along.
And in the glimmer of the moonlight they like to sing
   this song . . .

PAUL

Ah.
   (mocking) Our song.

For a second it seems that Paul is going to ask Jessie to dance, but he leans past her and takes Mabel's hand. The two make their way onto the small dance floor and begin a slow fox-trot.

If you like a ukulele lady
Ukulele lady like you . . .

But what they make of it is incredible—swooping, spinning, in perfect sync. Everyone's eyes turn to them and they accept the spotlight, familiar with it.

JESSIE

Wow.

Norman can feel himself shrinking beside her as they both stare at Paul's amazing grace. Surreptitiously, Norman turns to watch her profile, so young and beautiful it makes him ache. Forcing himself, he murmurs:

NORMAN

I am nowhere near as good as my brother . . .

Jessie turns, surprised. He smiles, trying to cover his struggle.

NORMAN

But would you do me the honor . . . ?

Charmed, touched by his confession, Jessie rises, fitting neatly into his outstretched arms, and they begin to dance, slowly, swaying, her hair brushing his face. Tentatively, he squeezes her closer and she responds, nestling into him. A blissful smile grows on his face as he breathes in the perfume of her body, and Paul and Mabel careen by unnoticed, the crooner crooning on, soft and mellow.

66. INT. BURNS HOUSE—DAY. *Jessie sits down in a chair next to a window and opens a letter with great curiosity. She reads it to herself.*

JESSIE

Dear Jessie, I cannot sleep. The moon is setting behind the Bit-
terroots. We are still dancing. Norman.

*Charmed, impressed, she smiles warmly, reading it over. A telephone rings, loud and
sharp, shattering the silence.*

Cut to:

67. *INT. THE MANSE—NIGHT. The phone rings again. A light snaps on. Norman,
in his underwear, hurries down to the phone, stumbling, snatches it up and answers
fuzzily:*

NORMAN

Yes . . . ?

*A low voice can be heard on the phone. Norman immediately looks awake and
worried.*

NORMAN

What's wrong . . . ?

MOTHER

Norman . . . ?

NORMAN *(to Mother)*

Just—wait . . .
    (into phone) Oh. Yes, I'm . . . I'm on my way . . .

MOTHER

Norman . . . ?

He hangs up, very worried now, and calls; hurrying up the stairs.

Norman and the police sergeant.

NORMAN

It's alright, Mother. It was . . . Go back to bed now, it's late . . .

68. EXT. POLICE STATION—NIGHT. *Norman hurries up the steps, tucking his shirt in.*

69. *INT. POLICE STATION—NIGHT. Norman arrives at the sergeant's desk out of breath, holding up his wallet. The sergeant waves it off.*

SERGEANT

Nah. He doesn't have to post bond. He covers the police beat and has friends here. All you have to do is look at him and take him home.

NORMAN

What'd he do?

SERGEANT

He hit a guy and the guy is missing a couple of teeth.

NORMAN

Why did he hit him?

SERGEANT *(holds up arrest sheet)*

It says here, "A remark was passed concerning the Indian he's with."

NORMAN *(relieved)*

Well, then he deserved it.

SERGEANT

It's not so funny. It's gonna cost your brother a lotta money to get out of this.

NORMAN

Why?

SERGEANT

A second guy is suing him.

NORMAN *(feeling a chill)*

What for?

Setting up the cell scene.

SERGEANT

For breaking up the place. He owns the restaurant.

(eyes Norman, hard) We're picking your brother up too much lately.

(Norman registers surprise) Besides, he's behind in the big stud poker game at Lolo. It's not healthy to get behind in the big game at Lolo. You guys think you're tough because you're street fighters, and Paul's got that right hand of his. But down there they don't play games like fistfighting. Down there it's stud poker and all that goes with it.

He stares meaningfully at Norman, who asks, weakly:

NORMAN

Is he hurt?

SERGEANT

Nah. He's not hurt, he's just sick. He drinks too much. Down at
Lolo they don't drink too much.

Feeling the chill rise inside of him, Norman can only stare back in silence. The sergeant holds him another beat, then relents.

SERGEANT

You better go take your brother home.

70. INT. CELL BLOCK—NIGHT. Chilled to the bone with fear now, Norman pushes the big door open and walks past the cells, peering in. From somewhere a drunk is singing "Ma, He's Making Eyes at Me." Paul is in the last cell. Norman stops a distance from it and studies his brother sitting on a mattressless bunk, right hand over his face, the knuckles cut and bleeding, as if hiding from the demeaning scene. Only when Norman steps closer does he see Mabel sprawled at Paul's feet. Her beautiful legs are splayed out, useless. Her stockings are hanging down. Her glistening hair lies across the floor, soaked in what is unmistakably vomit.

Norman can only stare a moment, stunned by the impact of the scene. Then he reaches for the latch, glancing over at the jailer, who nods. Norman opens the door and walks in. The smell weakens his knees. He gasps, involuntarily holding his breath.

The CREAK of the DOOR seems to wake Mabel. She looks up dully. Norman turns to Paul, not sure what to say, but Paul's face remains hidden behind his hand. Norman's attention is taken by Mabel, who is struggling to rise.

Norman watches her legs buckle again and again, and finally she falls back, rolling in the vomit, helpless. Norman winces, looks to Paul for help, but Paul doesn't move, doesn't look. Norman sighs, and heaves her up. She's heavy and awkward and the best he can do is drag her out, her toes bumping against the rough floor. After she is well down the hall, Paul rises and follows like a ghost, his hand still over his face.

71. EXT. CAR—NIGHT. It drives down a dark road.

[103]

Brad Pitt between takes.

72. INT CAR—NIGHT. Norman is at the wheel. Next to him Mabel lies in a crumpled heap, her breathing heavy. Behind, Paul sits, wrapped in silence. After a long tense moment, Norman finally speaks.

NORMAN

If you need any money, Paul . . .

No response. He glances back. Paul is barely visible in the shadows. His hand is still over his face. Norman adds meaningfully:

NORMAN

or anything else . . . I want you to know . . .

PAUL *(very quiet)*

She lives past the slaughterhouse.

Norman's voice hardens slightly with frustration.

NORMAN

I can *help.*

No response. His teeth clench in anger. Then:

PAUL

Turn here.

Norman sighs, and turns down the dark, rutted road.

73. EXT. PAVILION—DAY. A church picnic is in full swing. Meat sizzles over a grill. Food of every description covers the picnic tables. Children run around dirtying their Sunday clothes. A large group is gathered by a horseshoe pit, watching the Reverend play, his movements as elegant and disciplined as if he were casting. All the while Mother whispers to Norman.

MOTHER

. . . Cynthia McNulty passed. You remember her, big woman, hennaed her hair. There, that's . . . ohh, what an angel. That's Mary Beth Hoyt's newest. She had him in a hospital, can you believe it? Croupy, but I fixed him a plaster . . .
   (to woman welcoming Norman) Ethel. Thank you. Oh, yes, we're very proud of him . . .
   (laughs, whispers) Her daughter has turned into quite a beauty. There. In the sailor suit. Twenty just a week ago. Bright as a light, Norman . . .

And then, suddenly Paul materializes, strong and golden, as if nothing bad had ever happened to him. He strides toward the horseshoe pit, not noticing Norman and Mother yet. All eyes seem to turn to him and he smiles his sunniest smile as the con-

Clara and Norman at the picnic.

gregation greets him, young women especially, and the Reverend turns and sees him. Norman can't miss the look, surprise and pleasure, in the Reverend's face.

Then Paul's eyes meet Norman's. His smile stiffens. An edge of shame sweeps his face, even anger, and he turns quickly away, making clear to Norman that he wants to avoid him. Norman keeps looking at him with a mixture of anger and concern, confused as always by his brother. During this, Mother has gone on, oblivious.

MOTHER

Mr. Murchison, how are you?
  (loud) How are you? No. No, this is Nor-man. Yes, hasn't he grown up . . . ?!

And a rough old hand pinches Norman's cheek, pulling his attention away from the scene. Norman turns to greet the smiling deaf man, who has brown spittle from a wad of tobacco dribbling down his cheek. Then an "Ooooooh!" goes up from the crowd. Norman and Mother both turn just as Paul throws a beautiful, floating shoe high in

Clara and Paul.

the air for a perfect ringer. Applause, cheers. The Reverend's face lights up with pride. Mother's face lights up with delight.

MOTHER

Paul's here . . . !

Taking Norman's arm she hurries forward, but Norman holds back, forcing a smile.

NORMAN

I can't. Sorry. I have to go meet Jessie Burns' family.

MOTHER *(immediately interested)*

Oh?

The reverend and Paul play horseshoes.

NORMAN

They're driving in to the station. Her brother is coming home.
From California.

MOTHER

Oh. Well, now . . .
   (wicked) Should we have this girl over to dinner, Norman?

NORMAN *(smiles back)*

Could be, Mother.

*Laughing, she moves to the group surrounding Paul. Norman stands another moment,
watching his brother, then walks away.*

Extras on the bank of the Yellowstone River.

74. EXT. TRAIN PLATFORM. Norman hurries in nervously buttoning his jacket, carrying a bouquet. It is not difficult to spot the BURNS FAMILY *in a huge, excited gaggle, carrying baskets of food and peering anxiously down the tracks.*

NARRATOR

The Burns family were a poor family. Mr. Burns ran a general store in a one-store town and still managed to do badly. They were Methodists, a denomination my father always referred to as "Baptists who could read." But I found them as surprising and delightful, and as overwhelming, as Jessie herself.

Jessie sees Norman and beams, unguardedly happy.

JESSIE

Here's Norman!

Immediately, the whole family descends on him, sweeping him up as one of their own. Overwhelmed, Norman hands Jessie the flowers.

AUNT SALLY

Oh, *flowers* . . .

JESSIE

Oh, thank you. This is my father. Norman. Aunt Sally. Uncle Jimmy. My little brother, Ken. Where's Mother? Mother, this is Norman . . .

MRS. BURNS

They're beautiful. We should find some water before they wilt . . .
    (to Norman) Very pleased to meet you. Jessie tells me you're a poet . . .

JIMMY *(through it all)*

He's due in at five seventeen. They're usually right on the mark. Maybe a minute off, maybe two . . .

MR. BURNS

Are you related to the fishing newspaperman?

NORMAN

My brother.

AUNT SALLY

Jessie says you just got your degree.

Norman meets Neal Burns.

NORMAN

Yes.

AUNT SALLY *(continuing)*

With that kind of education you can do anything. Jessie, you know, was at the university. She was majoring in . . .

JESSIE *(referring to Paul)*

A darb.

KEN

Flapperism.

AUNT SALLY

Political science, I believe, wasn't it? But she dropped out.

JESSIE

Aunt *Sally* . . .

AUNT SALLY

She could learn from you—stick-to-ativity . . .

MRS. BURNS

Let him breathe. He's not used to all of this. He's a Presbyterian.

Norman bursts into laughter with the others, surprising himself, beginning to relax in the ease of their warmth.

Then a WHISTLE BLARES. *Instantly, Norman is forgotten.*

The whole clan turns anxiously toward the tracks where a locomotive is pulling in. Steam fills the station, and as it clears, everyone sees NEAL BURNS, *twenty-five, handsome but slightly dissipated, step off the train, wearing white flannels and two tennis sweaters. Norman's eyes narrow as he sizes Neal up quickly.*

NARRATOR

Jessie's brother, Neal, stepped off the train trying to remember what he thought a Davis Cup tennis player looked like, which struck me as odd, especially since you couldn't jump over a tennis net in Wolf Creek without landing in cactus. But then he recognized his relatives, and realizing he couldn't be Bill Tilden or F. Scott Fitzgerald anymore, he simply turned his profile and waited to be kissed.

The clan covers him, the women hugging and kissing him, Norman seeing with a pang how accepting and expressive their love for this bloated pretender is. Grinning like a little girl, Jessie pulls Neal to Norman.

JESSIE

Neal, this is Norman Maclean.

NEAL *(shakes hands, suave and phony)*

Old boy . . .

Norman's smile hardens with dislike, but the troupe sweeps past him, not noticing, leaving Norman alone with Neal's suitcase which sits forgotten, and Norman sees that it is a battered affair, its straw sides breaking open, one of its clasps gone. Surprised, even touched, he picks it up and follows the raucous group out.

75. EXT. *BURNS HOUSE*—DAY. *Lights are on all over the rambling, weathered farm-house. Loud, happy voices can be heard from inside as scruffy chickens peck around the front yard.*

76. INT. *BURNS DINING ROOM*—DAY. *The women are cleaning up the dinner dishes as Mr. Burns calls:*

MR. BURNS *(v.o.)*

A toast! Come on . . . !

The women take off their aprons and start in, deep in discussion.

AUNT SALLY

Does he look pale to you, Flo?

MRS. BURNS

I thought they had sun in California . . .

AUNT SALLY

But he has his appetite, thank God . . .

MRS. BURNS *(pleased)*

Yes. Yes, he does . . .

They enter living room.

MR. BURNS *(to Norman)*

With all the famous people he knows, I thought he could get my hardball autographed. I sent it out there. I know the Babe's been out there in the pictures, but Neal couldn't get to him, I guess. I heard he's even got bodyguards. Him and Dempsey. What does Dempsey need with a bodyguard, anyway . . . ?

JIMMY *(to Neal)*

So, what was the first stop? I remember when I travelled out there, it was San Berdoo. San Berdoo, then the desert. Hell of a lot of desert. And of course Salt Lake. You'd change in Salt Lake. There was a hotel nearby, served oysters of all things . . .

The women walk in.

MRS. BURNS

Oh, not the homemade beer

NEAL *(murmurs)*

Joy.

Mr. Burns pops the cap and beer erupts, splashing everyone.

KEN

Down in the trenches . . . !

MRS. BURNS

Get me a towel, dear . . .
      (Sally gets a towel)

MR. BURNS *(licking his fingers)*

Mm. A good year.

Laughter. Mr. Burns fills everyone's glass.

MRS. BURNS *(to Ken, who holds out glass)*

Ah—ah . . .

SALLY

Do you drink, Norman?

MR. BURNS

Just a drop, Flo . . .

JESSIE *(smiling)*

A tiny bit . . .
(*Norman smiles back*)

Then Neal holds up his glass and everyone stops.

NEAL

Well. To the famdamily.

Everyone drinks. Neal makes a small, disgusted face at the beer and heads to the liquor cabinet, pouring himself a drink. Norman notices everyone tense, fills the silence with an innocuous question.

NORMAN

How long are you planning to stay?

Neal turns to him for the first time and smiles.

NEAL

Sport. Sport, c'mere. C'mere . . .

Wagging, the dog trots over to him.

NEAL

I don't know.

He begins tussling with Sport, looking at no one else.

NEAL

I miss the ocean.

JESSIE *(hopping on it)*

What's it like?

NEAL

Big. Blue. People ride on the waves. They . . . Let go, let go!
  (he pulls hand out of Sport's mouth) They swim out and pick the
biggest wave. It's always the sixth.

NORMAN *(automatically)*

Seventh.

*Neal ignores this, tussles harder with Sport, working him into a frenzy. Jessie reaches
out as if to stop him.*

NEAL

And they lie on top of it and just coast in. I got pretty good at it.
Ow! *Dammit.* Bad! Bad dog!

He slaps Sport smartly across the nose.

NEAL

Jeez, Ma.

MRS. BURNS *(miserable)*

You get him excited . . .

Poor Sport slinks away on his belly. Neal pours another drink and Norman eyes him coldly, liking him less every minute.

NEAL

Anyhoo. What was I saying?

MR. BURNS

The ocean . . .

JESSIE

The water . . .

AUNT SALLY

Waves . . .

NEAL

Yeah. We'd ride those waves all day, all the boys . . . Ramon, me, Ronnie Coleman. I got pretty good. . . .

AUNT SALLY *(amazed)*

I can't picture Ronald Coleman riding on waves.

Jessie bursts into laughter, unable to stop herself. And the rest join in, somewhat hysterically and with great relief. Disconcerted for only a moment, Neal joins them.

NEAL

Some Kodak, hey? Yeah, well . . .

He stretches and takes a step toward the door. Norman sees the pained expressions on the whole family. Then, suddenly, Mrs. Burns blurts:

MRS. BURNS

Maybe you could go fishing with Norman sometime . . . ?

Both Neal and Norman stop, at a complete loss. The family brightens, looking hopefully at Norman.

NORMAN

Oh. Yeah . . .

MRS. BURNS

Wonderful. Wouldn't that be . . . ?

NEAL

Fishing?

NORMAN *(dry, challenging)*

You *do* fish?

EVERYONE

Sure he does. Yes. Who doesn't?

NEAL

Oh, you betcha.

MRS. BURNS

So. When would be a good time for you, Norman?

NORMAN

Uh . . . Well . . . Friday?

EVERYONE

Friday's good. Fine, etc. What time?

NORMAN

Say about—six?

NEAL

A.M.?

Everyone laughs as if it's a joke.

MRS. BURNS

He'll be there, won't you, honey? That's so very, very kind of
you, Norman.

JESSIE

And maybe Paul could come, too?

FATHER

And *how*.

NORMAN

Paul? Oh . . .
   (dry) I'm sure he'd love to.

*Buzzing happily, the table breaks up, enabling Neal to pass out the door, except that
Jessie and her mother are fully aware of his exit. They pass a significant glance to each
other as Mrs. Burns walks into the kitchen. A beat, then Jessie looks up at Norman,
tough, straight, hopeful.*

JESSIE

Why don't you go with Neal, Norman?

NORMAN

Hm?

From left: Ken (David Creamer), Uncle Jimmy (John Reubens), and Neal (Stephen Shellen).

JESSIE

To make your plans.

He gets it. His shoulders droop. He nods.

NORMAN

Oh. Sure. I'd love to.

77. *EXT. BLACK JACK'S BAR—DAY. A car sits in front of the dilapidated ex-boxcar stuck on the edge of the hamlet. A crude sign reads, "BLACK JACK'S."*

78. *INT. BLACK JACK'S BAR—MIRROR—DAY. In a wavy mirror is a reflection of Neal, looking back intently at his face as his mouth moves between drinks.*

It was an otter and her pups. I had a hard time trailing them because they turn white in the winter. Anyhoo, I trailed them all day right up to the top of Rogers Pass, where, did you know this? There's a thermometer up there that's stuck, this is official, at 69 degrees below zero . . .

Norman, next to Neal, rolls his eyes and sips at the horrible moonshine. A frail, trembling old barkeep leans against the split-log bar.

NARRATOR

After a few shots of the especially vile whiskey brewed by old Black Jack himself, Neal began to hold forth. He'd chosen Montana subjects to spin his pointless lies about, shooting, hiking, trapping, probably, I figured, to impress the only other client at the bar, whom he had particularly ignored so far, a ploy that was beginning to pay off.

NEAL

She tried to shake me again and again, and when she couldn't she gnawed a couple of trees down across the path to stop me. Now, night was coming on, and it was so cold, the wool in my coat was turning stiff. I couldn't feel my hands. I was thinking about my dog, Sport, who was with me. I was thinking, if it gets much worse I just might have to slit him open and stick my hands inside to keep them from freezing. I'd done it before, up near the Yukon.

At the end of the bar sits a thirty-year-old woman, pretty, tough, staring at Neal's profile, very interested.

NARRATOR

The woman Neal was not looking at went by the name of Old Rawhide. About ten years before she'd been elected Beauty Queen of Wolf Creek. She'd ridden bareback standing up through the one hundred and eleven inhabitants, mostly male. Her skirts flew high and she won the contest. But since she didn't have what it takes to become a professional rider, she did the next best thing. However, she still wore the divided skirts of a horsewoman, although they must have been a hardship in her new profession.

NEAL

It would've been a tough thing to do. Sport means more to me than I can say, but when you're cold and starved for so long, then your mind does funny things. Finally, it got so dark I couldn't see my nose in front of my face. A wind came up. Snow was blowing into my eyes. And then I took a step, and the ground just wasn't there. I grabbed a branch, and hung, suspended over a two-hundred-foot chasm. And then I heard something. A kind of growling, and I looked up, and there, stretched out on a branch ready to pounce on the first deer that came along was the otter . . .

RAWHIDE *(unable to stand it)*

Hey, buster. What are otters doin' on the top of Rogers Pass? I thought they swam down in the cricks.

Neal stops in midsentence and, not turning his head, finally looks at RAWHIDE *in the mirror, transforming himself at once into F. Scott Fitzgerald. With a small, suave smile, he says to* BLACK JACK, *his voice beginning to slur with drink:*

NEAL

Jack—give the lady a whiskey . . .

And Rawhide slides eagerly across the intervening packing-crate stools until she bumps into Norman, giving him an ugly look.

Rawhide (Susan Traylor) listens dubiously to Neal's stories.

NORMAN

Yeah. Well, I gotta shove off . . .

He finishes the last of his glass, shivers at the foul brew, and starts off. Rawhide slips into his seat, smiling seductively at Neal's profile. At the door, Norman can't resist:

NORMAN

Don't forget, fishing Friday. Old boy . . .

In the mirror he sees Neal blink, looking up blankly for Norman's face.

NEAL

What . . . ?

And Norman exits, thoroughly disgusted.

Norman asks Paul to go fishing.

79. *INT. THE MONTANA CLUB—DAY. It is a large, dim room with a bar at the end. Only a scattering of men are there, including Paul, who sits alone, concentrating over a notebook, drink in hand. It isn't until Norman stops before him that Paul looks up, and Norman sees the unguarded surprise and guilt in his expression.*

PAUL

Brother . . .

NORMAN

They told me at the paper you'd be in your other office.

PAUL

Deadline. I can't work there . . .

NORMAN

Yeah.

Casting around, Paul forces a smile.

PAUL

Come up for a drink . . . ?

Norman holds his eye a moment longer, as if deciding whether to talk about jail. Then he relents and shrugs.

NORMAN

A favor.

PAUL *(great relief, wry)*

Uh-oh.

NORMAN

Go fishing with me.

PAUL *(surprise, then, happy)*

Done.

Without thinking, he leads Norman to the bar.

NORMAN

And . . .
(*sighs*) Jessie's got a brother. He's in from California . . .

PAUL

Uh-oh.

He signals the bartender, who pours two drinks beneath the bar and serves them as Norman goes on happily.

NORMAN

And I said I'd take him fishing—with *us*. I won't lie to you. He's a world-champion pigfucker.

PAUL *(smiles)*

Bait fisherman.

NORMAN

He didn't say.

PAUL

He'll show up with a coffee can full of worms. Red can. Hills Bros. coffee. I'd lay a bet on it.

He holds out his hand as if to bet. Norman sighs, admits:

NORMAN

I promised Jessie.

PAUL

Ah.
   (eyes Norman) Are you getting serious?

NORMAN

I don't know. She . . .

PAUL

What?

Norman shakes his head, waving it away. Paul smiles, kindly.

PAUL

Well, then I guess we better do it.

Norman returns a smile of gratitude, his guardedness dissolving.

79A. EXT. FORK OF THE CLEARWATER—DAY. The sun beats down on the slow moving water. It is completely silent.

80. NEAL'S CAR—DAY. A cloud of dust rises. A horn honks in the distance, growing louder as a car appears out of the dust and drives up the bumpy road, revealing Neal, looking fuzzy in wilted clothes, pressing his hand to the horn. Then, out of the bushes step Paul and Norman, hot, angry, fed up, holding their hands out for Neal to stop. It takes a moment for him to focus and to comprehend. Then:

NEAL

Oh.

He stops honking, and Norman sees the top of another head slowly rise to reveal Rawhide.

PAUL

As I live and breathe.

She gives Paul a tough look, points a thumb at Neal.

RAWHIDE

Buster here wants to fish.

Neal, "Buster," is busy fumbling with something. The two men peer in to see a bottle of hooch and a bottle of strawberry pop, which Neal is splashing in the vicinity of a paper cup.

Stephen Shellen, Brad Pitt, Susan Traylor, and Craig Sheffer between takes.

PAUL

Yum.

NORMAN

You're late, Neal.

Neal's eyes take a while to focus.

NEAL

I . . . didn't get in till late . . .

PAUL

I didn't get in at *all*, but I was here.

Neal cowers slightly. Norman sighs.

NORMAN

Neal, Paul . . .

Paul takes Neal's hand and squeezes hard but speaks quietly.

PAUL

Neal, in Montana there are three things you're *never* late for—
church, work, and fishing.

Neal grimaces at the handshake, then points in the direction of Rawhide.

NEAL

Yeah. Rightyo. This, this is . . .

PAUL AND NORMAN

We've met.

*But Rawhide holds out her hand anyway. Norman, nearest, can't reach it. She
giggles.*

RAWHIDE

Don't go 'way . . .

*She steps out of the car and immediately begins weaving away, fighting to reach Nor-
man like someone climbing a mountain. Uncertain, Norman starts toward her, hand
remaining out, until she finally manages to reach and hold on tightly.*

RAWHIDE

Watch the first step, it's a lulu.

*And she breaks into disarming laughter, which infects both Norman and Paul, who
smile widely.*

PAUL

So.

NORMAN

Yeah, ah . . . you ready?

NEAL *(blank)*

What?

NORMAN

Fishing.

Rawhide sinks heavily to the running board, her skirt hiked up past her tattered stockings, and mumbles:

RAWHIDE

Buster wants to fish . . .

Neal nods in sage agreement, a pink mustache forming from his drink. Cheerfully, Paul calls out:

PAUL

Well, then—we're off! Oh, wait a minute. What about the bait, Neal?

NEAL *(brightens)*

Oh. Dumb Dora . . .

He fumbles in the backseat and comes up with a red Hills Bros. coffee can full of earth. Paul grins triumphantly at Norman.

81. EXT. RIVER—DAY. Paul and Norman walk along, waving at the flies. Norman says, miserable:

NORMAN

They're not gonna bite, anyway. It's too damn hot . . .

PAUL *(slaps fly)*

May he catch three doses of clap. Gee, I'm glad I didn't go home first and get some sleep.
(looks back) Where is he, anyway?

Norman looks back. Neither Neal nor Rawhide are present. Norman sags.

NORMAN

Aw . . .

82. EXT. DEAD HOLE—DAY. Looking everywhere, Norman toils up a rise and there below him sit Neal and Rawhide, on the edge of a "dead hole," a piece of the river not connected to the main body, its surface covered with scum.

NORMAN

What the *hell* are you . . . ?

He fights back his anger, conciliatory.

NORMAN

See, ah, this is what they call a dead hole, Neal. You can't . . .

NEAL

There are lots of fish.

Norman peers beneath the surface to see several mud-colored fish lying at the bottom.

NORMAN

Those are suckers.

NEAL

What's a sucker?

Rawhide laughs in disbelief. Norman rolls his eyes, disgusted.

RAWHIDE

Quick, Henry, the flit. . .

Norman turns back. Rawhide is waving vainly at the clouds of insects around her head as Neal reaches into the coffee can and comes up with a handful of wriggling worms. His brow knitted in concentration, he skewers the lot with his hook, then drops them into the tepid water. Norman can only stare as the botch of squirming pink sinks to the bottom, almost on top of the fish. Not one of them stirs. Norman tears his eyes away from this spectacle, hesitating, sure he shouldn't leave them, but finally shrugs.

NORMAN

Well . . . Good fishing . . .

NEAL *(foggily)*

What?

And Norman walks away, defeated.

83. EXT. THE RIVER—DAY. The river runs in waves and ripples and backwaters and little rapids, each with a different sound, a different motion, carrying itself on endlessly, the merciless sun glinting off its surface like diamonds. Paul appears, stepping out of the glare as he searches along the bank, finally smiling, seeing Norman asleep in the shade of a willow. Quietly, he crouches beside him and opens his creel. One sad fish lies in the fresh-picked laurel leaves. Norman opens his eyes.

NORMAN

I know. You have twenty.

Paul opens his creel. It's empty. They smile.

Brad Pitt.

PAUL

Did you find him?

NORMAN

Screw him.

Paul laughs. Norman struggles up, cranky and disgusted, brushing himself off.

PAUL

I thought we were supposed to help him.

NORMAN

How do you help that son of a bitch?

PAUL *(shrugs)*

By taking him fishing.

NORMAN

He doesn't *like* fishing. He doesn't like Montana, and he sure as
hell doesn't like *me.*

Paul smiles up at him, squinting against the sun. Then he says, thoughtful and quiet:

PAUL

Well . . . but maybe what he likes is somebody trying to help
him.

*Automatically, Norman begins to respond, aggravated, but then, comprehending the
words, he is brought up so sharply Paul can see it on his face as he stares back, surprised
at Paul's perception, both of them understanding that Paul was talking about himself
as well, baring himself for a brief moment in the hot shade of the willow. Then, with
the same serious expression, he breaks the moment:*

PAUL

Did you sink the beer?

And Norman answers just as seriously:

NORMAN

You bet your life.

*84. EXT. RIVER—DAY. Under the blazing sun, Norman hurries toward a deep, cold
hole, his mouth dust-dry. Behind him Paul strides, twirling a bottle opener on one
finger.*

Robert Redford gives direction between takes.

PAUL

I can taste it. I can *taste* it . . .

But Norman is stopped short, peering into the hole. Paul looks in after him. The hole is empty.

PAUL

Are you sure this is the right hole . . . ?

Norman nods, watching Paul's expression turn deadly with sudden comprehension. He gives Norman a hard look.

PAUL

Should we kill him?

85. EXT. RIVER—DAY. Both brothers stride angrily along. They round a bend and spot a nest of empty beer bottles near the mouth of the river.

Paul kicks viciously at them, sending them spinning against the rock. Then:

NORMAN

Holy Christ.

He is squinting at two bumps on a sandbar. Paul's eyes follow as Norman splashes toward them, and the bumps become first two rear ends raised to the sun, and then two bodies, naked, facedown, fast asleep, side by side, their clothes strewn about, signs of wild lovemaking in the sand. The last of the liquor and pop sizzle in the heat. The red can rests faithfully by Neal's side, its earth as cracked as Norman's lips, its color no brighter than the cruel blistering sunburn that covers both sleepers from the soles of their feet to the roots of their hair. Norman sucks in his breath.

NORMAN

Oh, shit.
   (sags) I think I'm in trouble.

PAUL *(arriving behind, peers closely)*

Hold on . . . She's got a tattoo.

NORMAN

Huh . . . ?

He looks closer and sees on one blazing buttock the letters LO and on the other VE.

PAUL

Initials?

NORMAN

No, look . . .

He points. Directly in the center, crossing from one cheek to the other, is a hyphen.

[136]

NORMAN

L O - V E. Love.

They look at each other and burst into laughter.

85A. EXT. THE CARS—DAY.

NEAL

Ahhhhhhhh!!!

He screams as Norman touched his inflamed skin, struggling to get his half-conscious body into his car. Behind them, Paul drops Rawhide, dressed only in her step-ins, onto the front seat of his car. Her reaction to the sunburn, however, is quite different. She pulls at Paul's arm with a slightly suggestive smile.

RAWHIDE

You got a drink, Buster?

PAUL *(laughs)*

Buster's the one with the red ass.

Laughing, Norman climbs into Neal's car.

NORMAN

I am in deep trouble.

PAUL

Want me to come along and protect you?

NORMAN

Perfect. I'm sure Mrs. Burns would love to meet the girlfriend.

RAWHIDE

I ain't burned. The sun don't bother me . . .

Norman starts the car, shaking his head ruefully. But Paul keeps watching him, then he shrugs, somewhat tentative.

PAUL

What the hell. Why don't I just stay over with you tonight at the folks? We can come back here tomorrow, wipe this day right off the books . . .

NORMAN *(smiles)*

It's a deal.

PAUL *(genuinely happy)*

Good. Good. But we should call Mother first. Y'know how excited she gets when I just walk in.

NORMAN

You call. She likes hearing from you.

They share a tender, understanding moment, but Rawhide bangs on the horn.

RAWHIDE

Busterrr, come *on*. I'm dry as dirt . . . !

PAUL

Hark. Fair Juliet speaks.

And they drive off, laughing. Paul hangs out the window and yells:

PAUL

Good luck, Brother!

Norman brings Neal home.

86. EXT. THE BURNS HOUSE—LATE DAY. Surreptitiously, Norman helps Neal up the front path from the car, Neal's face screwed into a mask of pain, clutching only a bunch of his clothes to his waist, but the flexing of his knee to reach the porch step is too much.

NEAL

Ahhhhh!

NORMAN (cringing)

Shhhh!

Too late. Jessie and Florence stand at the door in horror.

FLORENCE

Sweet Jesus, what have you done to my boy?!

She runs to Neal, reaching out with two protective hands.

NORMAN

No, don't . . .

NEAL *(as she grabs him)*

AHHHHH!

Florence releases him in anguish and bewilderment.

NORMAN

He . . . fell asleep . . .

Norman turns Neal around, revealing the sunburn.

NORMAN

. . . in the sun.

FLORENCE

Oh, my Lord in Heaven . . . !

JESSIE

Naked?

Norman glances up at her, his expression pleading, but Jessie's horror has transformed into rage. She fixes him with merciless eyes.

JESSIE

You left him *alone.*

NORMAN

I . . .

As he struggles, Florence recovers, spiriting Neal gingerly inside, murmuring.

FLORENCE

Alright, honey. We'll fix it, we'll fix it . . .

NORMAN

. . . he was, he brought someone along, and . . .

JESSIE

You left him *alone.*

NORMAN

No, you see . . . he . . . I . . .

But Jessie has already turned on her heel and walked inside, slamming the door behind her. Sighing, Norman knocks on it. Jessie opens it, her face set and cold. Norman motions over his shoulder to Neal's car.

NORMAN

I . . . I need a ride home.

87. *INT./EXT. CAR/ROAD—LATE DAY. Norman sits humbly, watching the narrow road as Jessie drives Neal's open car. Her expression remains set. She doesn't speak. Norman steals a look at her—short hair blowly slightly, a slender hand shifting the gears competently, delicate knees showing beneath her skirt. They turn into the deep canyon and Jessie slows. Up ahead two cars sit stranded in deep water that covers the road. Norman looks for her reaction. A beat, then her face hardens with determination. She speaks, quietly.*

Jessie drives Norman home.

JESSIE

You'd better hold on.

And suddenly, she veers off the road and straight up the canyon side, lurching over the rocks and ravines. Norman, almost tossed out, grabs onto the seat.

88. INT./EXT. CAR/TRACKS—LATE DAY. *They crest a rise and railroad tracks come* INTO VIEW. *With her thin arms, she fights the big steering wheel and muscles the car right onto the roadbed, flooring it. Norman's hat blows off. He grabs it, clamps it down. The car speeds up, every piece of metal in it rattling in concert with the ties. He shouts over the noise, trying to chuckle.*

Filming the drive home.

NORMAN

Um . . . Got a train schedule . . . ?

All she has is a small smile on her face. Clearly, she is enjoying the ride and Norman's discomfort.

NORMAN

You know . . .
   (leans closer) You know . . . when I worked for the Forest Service? We'd send freight trains down this way, any old time. Big, you know, a hundred cars full of logs, and the hell with the schedule . . . !

Before he finishes they are suddenly engulfed in a tunnel. For a moment there is only darkness and a ROAR *of the* ENGINE *and a* WHOOSH *of the* WIND. *Then they're out.*

Jessie.

88A. EXT. TUNNEL/TRESTLES—LATE DAY. The clear blue sky surrounds them on both sides. Norman looks down and sees the girders of an immense trestle stretching to the river far, far below. He gasps in shock. The WIND WHISTLES *into his mouth. His hat flies off unheeded. He grabs the side of the car with all his strength, his knuckles whitening. Angry, he turns to Jessie, but sees her caught in the light, her profile clear, her eyes snapping with intensity and spirit, her hair swirling like a dark halo. She is smiling, wide and open, no longer just showing off, but truly joyous, and Norman forgets his fear and stares at her, enraptured by her strength and her beauty, feeling himself beginning to smile, too, hearing himself laugh, happy and wild and unfettered, as the car sizzles along the gleaming track.*

89. EXT. THE MANSE—TWILIGHT. The car pulls up. Inside, Jessie and Norman sit, their hair in wild tangles.

Then, tilting her head back, she shakes it hard, settling the hair into a perfect, gleaming cap.

Norman, pierced by the beauty of it, tries but can't summon words to express himself. Silent, he gets out, but can't let her go. He holds onto the car, and quips:

NORMAN

Thanks for the flight.

He is rewarded by a slight smile.

JESSIE

You're funny.

NORMAN *(hopeful)*

What's funny about me?

She looks at him a moment, her expression softening. Then:

JESSIE

You don't like my brother, do you?

He is about to lie gallantly, but can't, so he faces her.

NORMAN

No. I do not like your brother.

He sees her face harden.

NORMAN

I'm sorry. I don't know any card tricks. But I like *you*, Jessie. I want to see you again.

She colors, her expression uncertain. Trying to cover his desire with lightness, he asks:

NORMAN

Can't I like you and still not like your brother?

Before she can respond, Paul's car flies around the corner and stops inches before her bumper. He asks, honestly concerned:

Paul.

PAUL

How's your brother coming along?

JESSIE

You both left him *alone*.

PAUL *(sincerely contrite)*

I'm sorry. It was my fault.

JESSIE

You're not forgiven.

PAUL *(playful)*

Well . . . but is Norman forgiven?

Jessie looks at Norman, gauging him, enjoying the moment. Then she says, coolly:

JESSIE

Norman's not funny.

And she roars off, almost hitting Paul, who leaps onto his running board, impressed. Norman stares down the road at the disappearing Jessie, baffled.

90. INT. DINING ROOM—NIGHT. *The family sits around the dining table, Mother close to Paul.*

MOTHER

. . . and I hung fresh towels for you over the washstand . . .

PAUL

You mean you didn't powder my toothbrush, Mother?

Everyone chuckles.

REVEREND

Now, let Paul tell us his latest story, Clara . . .

PAUL

Which one, the murder, the fire, or the car wreck?

Mother tsks.

REVEREND

I think they should give you the church beat.

PAUL

Yes. Quote—the Reverend Maclean had quite a nice roast while dining with his family, all but the poor elder son enjoying themselves immensely . . .

Norman looks up, distracted, still thinking of Jessie.

MOTHER

What's wrong, Norman?

PAUL

He's not funny enough.

MOTHER

Pardon me?

REVEREND

There are more important accomplishments, Norman.

Norman tries to stop the joke that Paul has begun, but Paul rolls right along.

PAUL

Yes. So what if you're dull?

MOTHER

No. We're very proud of you.

PAUL *(comes in fast, in control)*

Alright, I do have one. No murder, no mayhem. I interviewed— *(pauses for effect)* the President.

Amazement.

PAUL

Yes, no, I did. He was in Dakota—fly fishing.

Murmurs: "No." "Calvin Coolidge?" "I don't believe it," etc.

PAUL

Yes. Calvin Coolidge. Wearing a suit and tie, white gloves and patent-leather shoes.
    (laughs all around) I asked him, "What're they biting on, sir?" and he said, "The end of my line."
    (big laughs) And then a bunch of locals ran up and stuck some newfangled fly on the size of a chicken, and old Cal heaved it out there, figured if he couldn't catch a trout, he could scare one to death . . .
    (big laughs) Yep. It'll be in the Sunday supplement—"Closed Mouth Cal Communes with the Crappies."

Laughter. The house seems filled with warmth. A beat of this, then Paul stretches.

PAUL

Ohhhh. That was *amazing*, Mother.

NORMAN

Usually, he eats what he can hit on the road.

Everyone laughs happily.

MOTHER

I do worry about your . . .

PAUL

Well, I think I'll run over . . .

MOTHER

Hm?

PAUL

I was just gonna say, I guess I'll look up some old pals, I'm in town and all . . .

MOTHER

Oh.

They look at him.

PAUL

Don't wait up . . .
  (smiles, points to roast) I'll eat the rest of that later, when no-body's looking . . .

And he leaves. The mood changes immediately, deflating, empty, worried, the joy gone with Paul. The Reverend breaks into the silence.

REVEREND

Did you hear that he's changed the spelling of our name?
  (starts away) MacLean, with a capital L. Now everyone will think we're Lowland Scots . . .

Then he walks away, leaving Norman and Mother in unhappy silence.

91. *INT. UPSTAIRS HALL—MORNING. In his bathrobe, Norman walks from his room to Paul's and opens the door. The bed is untouched. Paul is not there.*

92. *EXT. THE MANSE—MORNING. It is later. Norman sits on the porch glider, drink-ing coffee, absently staring out, worried and thoughtful. The old, odd mailman ap-pears, climbing the porch steps familiarly.*

Tom Skerritt and Robert Redford in the reverend's study.

MR. SWEENEY

Norman.

NORMAN

Hello, Mr. Sweeney.

He takes a bunch of mail out of his pouch.

MR. SWEENEY

Who do you know at the University of Chicago?

Surprised, Norman takes a letter from him.

MR. SWEENEY

Chicken in the car and the car won't go, that's how you spell Chi-car-go . . .

Distracted, Norman smiles. Mr. Sweeney waves.

MR. SWEENEY

Tomorrow.

Norman nods, friendly, but the moment he's alone, he tears the envelope and reads the letter: "Dear Mr. Maclean, As chairman of the English Department, it gives me great pleasure to accept your application and to offer you the position of instructor, beginning fall term. Your outstanding record, etc. . . ."
   Norman takes a deep breath, then grins, then looks slightly unsure, as he goes inside.

93. INT. THE MANSE—MORNING. He heads for the study where the Reverend's voice can be heard practicing a sermon. Norman pushes the open door wider, about to tell his father, but at the last moment, he decides against it. Not hearing him, the Reverend keeps on, his head buried in a book, reciting softly.

REVEREND

. . . Not in entire forgetfulness,
And not in utter nakedness,
But trailing clouds of glory do we come,
From God, who is our home . . .

Then without thinking, Norman speaks up.

NORMAN

Though nothing can bring back the hour
Of splendor in the grass, of glory in the flower,
We will grieve not, rather find
Strength in what remains behind . . .

Smiling, the Reverend joins in the game.

REVEREND

In the primal sympathy,
Which having been must ever be . . .

NORMAN

In the soothing thoughts that spring
Out of human suffering . . .

REVEREND

In the faith that looks through death.

Moved, the men look at each other, then Norman finishes, quietly:

NORMAN

Thanks to the human heart by which we live,
Thanks to its tenderness, its joys, and fears,
To me the meanest flower that blows can give
Thoughts that do often lie too deep for tears.

He stops. Nothing more is said. The two men remain, studying each other, the Reverend with a musing, appreciative smile, Norman feeling very strongly the emotion of the piece, the significance of the moment.

94. *EXT. TRAIN STATION PLATFORM—NIGHT. The Burns clan swarms around Neal, almost smothering him. Norman pushes his way through the crowd.*

It was a week, seven days exactly, before I spoke to Jessie again. She called to tell me that Neal was better, and had decided to go back to his life in California. *And* that he would appreciate me seeing him off. Though I was surprised by the request, I asked only one question of Jessie—Did *she* want me to come. And she answered, Yes.

Norman picks Jessie out of the crowd and melts, as always. She looks particularly beautiful and vulnerable, her eyes bright with suppressed tears.

CONDUCTOR

Aboard!

MRS. BURNS

Oh . . .

JIMMY

Time's up . . .

SALLY

Dear me . . .

A sudden, desperate flurry runs through the group, but Neal stands his ground, milking the scene, allowing the women to hug and kiss him once more. They are talking very quietly, privately to him, one at a time, such things as: "Have a wonderful time." "If you need any money just write." "I know you'll do well." "We'll miss you." "Try not to drink too much . . ." Norman watches Jessie hold him as tightly as she can. He feels a pang, seeing the kind of unreserved love she feels for her brother. Then it is Florence's turn. With a tragic expression, she clings to her son.

The TRAIN CLANKS. *The car behind Neal begins to move. He steps back from Florence and, with all eyes on him, sticks up his arm and the handrail is magically there. He grasps it, swinging casually onto the platform, his Bill Tilden sweater draped over his shoulders, his Scott Fitzgerald profile carefully calculated.*

Then he sees Norman and holds up a hand. For the briefest moment a look of thanks crosses his face, unrehearsed, and suddenly Norman can't hate him anymore.

Following Neal's gesture, Jessie turns to see Norman waving back, and smiles warmly at him, forgiving all. Norman smiles back, aching with desire, but doesn't move to her, sensitive to the family's privacy. They all wave happily at the train yelling at the same time:

MRS. BURNS

Good luck, son! We're all rooting for you! Let us know how it goes! Good luck! Good luck!

JIMMY

Don't take any wooden nickels, kiddo! Hey! Don't take any wooden . . .
  (louder) I say, don't take any wooden nickels . . . !

MRS. BURNS

There are sandwiches in the bag! Your favorite! And coffee in the thermos! Make sure you rub the cocoa butter on your back every night, alright? Don't forget! Write us! I put stationery in your grip! We love you, dear! We love you! Good luck . . . !

AUNT SALLY

Sandwiches, yes! Chicken salad!

KEN *(laughing)*

I killed the chicken!

AUNT SALLY

And a slice of my pie, too! It'll keep you 'til Salt Lake! Good luck! Good luck!

JESSIE *(after she turns back from seeing Norman)*

Goodbye! I love you! Be good! You'll do fine! You'll be swell! I love you! I love you, Neal!

The train disappears in a cloud of smoke. A beat, then the women crumble, their facades dissolving. Jessie puts her arms around her mother and Florence buries her face in her daughter's shoulder and sobs. Norman looks on, touched by the scene, even envious of it.

95. *EXT. MISSOULA—LATE DAY. Norman and Jessie walk along the river, her expression pained, sad. After a long moment she murmurs:*

JESSIE

If he comes back next summer, will you try to help him?

NORMAN

If *you* want me to, Jessie, I'll try.

JESSIE

He won't come back.

Her chin quivers. She fights it.

NORMAN

But he'll be alright. He has friends out there . . .

JESSIE *(bitter)*

Who, Ronald Coleman?
   (shakes head) Why is it that people who need help the most won't take it?

Norman looks at her sadly, thinking of Paul, and answers simply:

NORMAN

I don't know, Jessie.

She looks at him helplessly, unable to stop the tears from filling her eyes.

JESSIE

I don't cry, Norman.

And the tears spill out. Norman reaches for his handkerchief and tenderly touches her wet cheeks. A beat, then, gently changing the subject:

NORMAN

Would you like to see something?

JESSIE

Only if it's something good.

Smiling, Norman takes out the University of Chicago letter and hands it to her.

NORMAN

Read . . . ?

She wipes at her tears and reads it in the light of a street lamp and Norman watches the sadness fade, replaced by delight. Unable to wait until she's done, he grins, excited:

NORMAN

What do you think?

She looks up at him, beaming, impressed, proud.

JESSIE

I think it's . . . the berries.

He laughs.

JESSIE

I think it's heaven. *Chicago.*

NORMAN

Have you ever been?

JESSIE

No. Not anywhere.
    (concedes) Helena.
    (beams) Congratulations.

NORMAN *(grinning)*

Thanks.
    (hesitating) Well, you know, it's . . .

JESSIE

What? Don't you want it?

NORMAN

Sure. Sure I do. God, the University of Chicago!

He walks away and back, grinning foolishly, then shakes his head.

NORMAN

It's just that I'm . . .
    (sags a bit) I don't know if it's my . . .
    (embarrassed) . . . calling.

JESSIE *(amused by word)*

Calling?
    (quickly) It is. You're a poet, Norman, and you'll be a wonder-
ful teacher, and your students will love you . . .

She laughs happily, but Norman can only smile, still troubled.

NORMAN

Well . . . the truth is . . . I'm not sure I want to leave.

JESSIE

Montana? It'll always be here, Norman.

NORMAN

Not Montana.

JESSIE *(laughing in disbelief)*

Then *what*?

NORMAN *(facing her, strong)*

I don't want to leave you.

JESSIE *(barely breathes)*

Oh.

They stand a moment, facing each other, overcome by their feelings. Then he reaches out to her and she presses into his arms, joyous, finding his lips and kissing him with all of her stored passion, their eyes shut against the world.

96. INT. SPEAKEASY—NIGHT. Norman bangs down the stairs, lordly with love. At the bar, Paul turns, surprised.

PAUL

Well, now . . .

NORMAN

Draw us up a couple boilermakers, Murphy. Toute sweet.

And he laughs happily, puzzling Paul. Then he turns to the bar, drops the shot glass of whiskey into the mug of beer and raises it high.

Jessie and Norman.

NORMAN

To . . .
(*boldly*) The *heart*, goddammit!

Laughs. Norman chugs the beer, ending with the shot glass on his tongue. Scattered applause. He bows as Paul smiles knowingly.

PAUL

Oh, Lordy.

And Norman beams, sliding the second boilermaker to Paul.

NORMAN

I am in love with Jessie Burns.

Norman sees a look of anger pass quickly across Paul's face. Then he shakes his head, forcing a smile.

PAUL

Jesus, Norm. With all the fish in the river.

NORMAN

Not like her.

PAUL *(murmurs)*

Right.

NORMAN *(a sudden edge)*

Not like her, Paul.

And Paul backs off, light and easy. He takes the boilermaker and tips it toward Norman.

PAUL

Congratulations.

Norman's smile returns as Paul downs the drink, leaving the shot glass on the tip of his tongue a second, then letting it drop. Instinctively, Norman reaches for it, but Paul's right hand is lightning fast, catching it with barely a move. Then Paul looks at Norman, his grin slightly strange, challenging.

PAUL

Well, then, let's get the hell out of here and go celebrate.

NORMAN *(grins back)*

Done.

97. *EXT. ROAD—NIGHT. Paul's car whizzes down a smooth dirt road, its headlights revealing the Burma Shave signs that Chub talked about.*

98. *INT. CAR—NIGHT. But Norman doesn't notice. He's high and happy and drinking deeply from a hip flask that passes between the brothers.*

> NORMAN
>
> Okay, here's one from the East, brand new, hot stuff—
>   *(sings)* Yes, we have no bananas, We have no bananas today! We have homegrown potahtoes, And vine-ripened tomahtoes . . .

Paul keeps his eyes on the road, his smile fixed.

> PAUL
>
> It's a stinker.

> NORMAN
>
> But, yes, we have no bananas, We have no bananas today!

> PAUL
>
> It stinks, Brother . . .

> NORMAN *(laughs)*
>
> What do you mean? It's a classic! Yes, we've got no bananas, We've got no . . .

Almost missing a turn in the dark, Paul cuts the wheel hard. The car swerves onto a smaller, rutted road, kicking up dust.

> NORMAN
>
> Where are we going?

Paul says nothing, keeps smiling. Norman takes another pull on the flask.

NORMAN

Paul? Where are we . . . ?

Then the lights of Lolo Hot Springs come into view. Norman stiffens. Paul turns to him with the same challenging smile.

PAUL

I figured you felt lucky tonight. I could use the luck . . .

Norman says nothing, just stares back in anger and disbelief.

PAUL

Oh, for Christ's sake, don't be the professor tonight.
  (smiles) Norm?
  (grins, challenging) Preacher?

Reluctant, but unable to resist Paul's challenge, Norman gets out of the car.

99. INT. LOLO—NIGHT. The atmosphere seems to reach out and throttle Norman. It is silent, deadly, almost evil. The long, worn room is filled with dangerous-looking men hunched over their cards and used-up whores waiting their turns. A few faces look over, appraising Norman coolly as he stands feeling a chill run up his spine. Then Paul is at his elbow leading him to a table.

PAUL

My gal Sal . . .

He signals a bar girl, who comes over.

Lolo Hot Springs.

PAUL

Get my brother a drink, okay? As a matter of fact, how about a round on me? He's in love.

But his breezy self-assurance fails in the room. Hard-boiled gamblers just eye him as if he doesn't belong. Norman notices and feels the chill inside of him growing. Still, smiling, Paul looks past Norman to a room beyond, inside of which is a table full of better-dressed men sitting before piles of greenbacks, their Stetsons cutting their faces in half. It is clearly the big stud game. Paul's smile changes, turning hungry. He pats Norman's shoulder as he rises.

PAUL

Hang on . . .
(calls) Take care of him, Sal . . .

*He saunters to the doorway. Norman turns to watch, comprehension dawning imme-
diately. Paul addresses the players at the table, especially a* DAPPER MAN *at their center. Throughout this scene, Norman is unable to hear the conversation, and can only
see pieces of Paul and the men.*

PAUL

What say, boys? Got an empty chair?

DAPPER MAN *(shakes head, level)*

Not for you, Paul.

PAUL *(laughs, too loud)*

Oh, c'mon pal. You know I'm good for it.

DAPPER MAN

Not for you, Paul.

WHORE *(v.o.)*

Whatcha want, honey?

Norman turns to see a whore sitting in Paul's chair.

NORMAN

Hm?

WHORE

You wanta play cards?
(slight, tired smile) You wanta go upstairs?

[165]

NORMAN

Oh . . . No, I . . .

Voices rise in the room. He turns back, leaning forward in frustration.

DAPPER MAN

Beat your feet, Paul. I mean it.

PAUL

Uh-uh. I'm *in*, goddammit . . .

DAPPER MAN *(cold, level)*

You're out . . .

And Sal steps in front of Norman with his drink.

SAL

A buck. Pauly said he's payin', but . . .

There is a scraping of chairs, cursing from the room. Norman is up and past Sal, his arm knocking over the drink. What he sees is a tableau—the men standing, glaring at Paul—all but the Dapper Man, who remains seated, calm, cold. A man at the door leans to Paul and whispers in his ear. Norman starts forward to help. Paul shrugs and smiles at the man.

PAUL

Okay, okay . . .
 (slight edge) Okay.

He turns away, his expression tight, and sees Norman walking to him. Quickly, he holds up both hands.

PAUL

Hang on, hang on.

He starts out, smile restored, shaking his head.

PAUL

Nothing. Games, Brother.

But Norman will not be persuaded this time. He grabs Paul's arm, hard.

NORMAN

I don't care, *brother*—we're getting the hell out of here. *Now.*

Paul puts up no resistance. He just smiles and shrugs, looking slightly away.

PAUL

Rightyo . . .

And he saunters out next to Norman, through the tables of staring gamblers. The Whore stretches her foot out to stop Norman, who brushes past.

100. EXT. LOLO—NIGHT. Norman strides angrily to the car. Something hits him on the back, hard. He spins, sees Paul standing by the door, pointing.

PAUL

My keys.

Norman sees the keys on the ground. He looks up at Paul, puzzled.

PAUL

I'm not leaving.

NORMAN

What?

PAUL

Look.
    (holds out hands) . . . these hands are hot, Norm. I can feel it.

NORMAN

What are you talking about? You can't go back in there . . . !

PAUL

I'll be fine.

NORMAN

But . . . they won't even let you play!

PAUL *(smiles, knowing)*

Yeah, they will.

NORMAN

With what money? I *know* you're in debt, Paul, up to your goddamn neck!

Paul's smile turns dangerous. He responds, tough.

PAUL

But it's my debt, Brother. *My* debt.

NORMAN

Jesus Christ!

He can think of nothing else to say.

NORMAN

Jesus *Christ* . . . !

He snatches up the keys, hops in Paul's car and starts away with a spurt of gravel. Then:

PAUL *(v.o.)*

Hey . . .

Norman looks back. Paul is running toward him.

PAUL

Hey!

Norman jams on the brakes. Paul catches up, panting.

PAUL

Hey . . .

He leans down, his expression changed, apologetic.

PAUL

We didn't get to fish again, I . . . Maybe we could go tomorrow . . .

Norman can only stare, dumbfounded by the request.

PAUL

Maybe Father could come with us . . .

He looks at Norman, almost pleading, trying the only way he knows to wipe the ugliness away. He adds, gently:

PAUL

You ask him . . .

Then he turns and walks back into the building, leaving Norman staring after him, confused and very scared.

101. EXT. MANSE—EARLY MORNING.

102. INT. KITCHEN—EARLY MORNING. The Reverend and Norman, in fishing attire, sit eating silently. Paul's place is empty. A tension fills the room as Mother hustles around cooking and serving, her mouth shut tight. Norman's fear for Paul rises. He looks up at his father, tempted to tell all. And then the door bangs open, and Paul walks in, bringing sunlight and happiness with him. Relieved and at a loss, Norman can only stare at his face, clean and untouched.

PAUL

Something smells *real* good!

And he sits right down. Proudly, Mother holds up a pan.

MOTHER

Muffins . . .

PAUL *(happily)*

Good morning, everybody . . . !
  (takes muffin) Perfect.

MOTHER

I'm so glad you could make it, what with work and everything . . .

PAUL *(at Norman)*

I wouldn't miss it.

REVEREND

What are you working *on*?
	(*hopeful, pleased*) Do you have a story for us, Paul?

PAUL

A story? Well . . . let me see . . .

He looks up, forming his thoughts. Into the silence Norman speaks up, tentative:

NORMAN

I have one.

He pulls out the Chicago letter.

NORMAN

I've been offered a job, teaching literature, at the University of
Chicago . . .

MOTHER (*amazed*)

Oh . . .

REVEREND (*stunned*)

Yes . . . ?

NORMAN

Starting fall term.

He hands the letter around and looks at them, sure.

NORMAN

I'm going to take it.

A moment's silent shock, then:

MOTHER

Oh, *Norman* . . .

But it is to the Reverend that Norman turns, seeking the ultimate approval, and the Reverend responds with a small, helpless smile, only able to repeat softly:

REVEREND

Well, I am pleased. I am pleased . . .
    (nodding) I *am* pleased.

PAUL

A professor? A real professor? Damnation.

Norman turns, surprised, to see Paul grinning with real delight, rising to the occasion, honestly pleased with his brother's success. Norman smiles warmly back, and Paul squeezes his arm, unashamed, looking straight at him.

PAUL

I am proud of you.

103. EXT. DRIVEWAY—DAY. The three men finish piling their equipment in the rumble seat and get in, still laughing and joking. Mother hands Norman the folding Kodak.

MOTHER

Be sure and take pictures.

PAUL

Contact!

He revs the engine. Smiling, Mother watches them wave gaily as they drive away, the Reverend looking young and carefree.

The brothers and their father leave the house to go fishing.

104. EXT. THE RIVER—DAY. The three men walk up to a clearing high above the river. They are easy, happy, light. The slope down is steep and treacherous. Without thinking, Paul starts down, then stops and looks back at the Reverend, who smiles and motions downstream.

REVEREND.

I believe the high road will suit me better.

Automatically, both boys deny his weakness, but the Reverend only smiles at them with a tinge of sadness.

REVEREND

There was a time.

And he starts off. They watch him a beat, then Paul calls.

Filming the final fishing scene.

PAUL

You'll make a killing . . . !

And then the Reverend is gone. Paul turns to Norman.

PAUL

He'll make a killing . . .

Norman smiles reassuringly. Paul hesitates, then says, gently:

PAUL

Let's fish together today.

Together they scramble down the bank to the end of the river. Paul wades into the mid-dle of the strong current. Norman looks after him, the sound of the river slowly im-pinging on his consciousness. His eyes lose their focus as he listens to the voices echoing in the empty canyon around him. It is both sad and beautiful. He feels gooseflesh rise on his bare arms.

Then an insect smashes into his mouth, pulling him back to the moment. He spits, wiping at it, and in his open palm is a yellow-striped fly, which suddenly rises from its seeming death and buzzes away. Norman smiles, finds a rock and sits down, rum-maging through his fly box until he comes up with an almost-perfect copy of the insect. Grinning now, he ties it to his line and steps toward the nearest hole, beginning the gentle movement of a cast. Before the fly hits, the dark head of a trout leaps out of the water, striking at it and missing.

NORMAN

Ha!

Impatient for victory, he casts again. This time the fly rests on the water like an insect trying to swim. A long beat, then the fly is taken, snatched, as the big trout dives with it, and Norman sets the hook, watching the tip of the rod bob madly with fight, and beyond it, standing in silence, is Paul, hands on hips. Even with a big lusty fish on the end of his line, Norman has time to notice that Paul's basket is empty. Grinning even wider than before, he plays the big fish until it is exhausted, and scoops it up with his net, trying to look casual.

PAUL

Not bad.

NORMAN *(shrugs)*

Medium.

He glances up, unable to keep smug victory out of his expression. Paul smiles wryly back.

PAUL

Alright, what are they biting on?

NORMAN *(torturing him)*

What? Louder . . . !

PAUL *(sigh)*

What are they biting on?!

His voice echoes. Satisfied, Norman calls back:

NORMAN

Bunyan bugs!

PAUL

Ah . . .

He takes off his hat, where he keeps all his flies, and Norman watches him turn it around and around fruitlessly. Finally, relenting:

NORMAN

I have another one . . .

PAUL

I'll get it . . .

He walks over and Norman holds out the fly with a triumphant grin.

NORMAN

Means' Bunyan Bug number two stone fly.

Smiling back, Paul takes the fly and begins tying it onto his line. Norman watches in silence, seeing his young, strong brother in the filtered light, hearing the voices in the water behind them. His expression softens, his smile grows gentle, and he says:

[176]

NORMAN

I'm going to ask Jessie to marry me.

He sees that pang of pain cross Paul's face, before he looks up, trying to smile.

PAUL

Quite a day . . .

Again, Norman speaks gently.

NORMAN

Come with us to Chicago.

But Paul turns away, busying himself with the fly. Norman sighs.

NORMAN

You can't stay here, Paul.
    (no response) Chicago's two thousand miles away. It has a dozen
papers. You can be right in the middle of things.
    (steels himself) Come with us.

Paul's back doesn't move. Norman takes a step toward him, adamant.

NORMAN

Let me help.

*He stares at the unmoving back, anger rising in him. Then Paul turns with a sweet,
accepting, sincere smile.*

PAUL

Oh . . . I'll never leave Montana, brother . . .

*And he starts away, heading upstream. Norman can only watch, his anger dissolving
with sad acceptance.*

[177]

The reverend reads his Greek bible.

105. EXT. THE RISE—DAY. Slowly, his feet heavy, Norman crests the rise and spots his father sitting on the edge holding a book.

Norman stands next to him, glancing down at the book, seeing that it is the Bible in Greek. The Reverend smiles vaguely at him, his eyes on Paul who is emerging at the roughest and wildest spot on the river. He watches Paul fix on the eddy in front of a rock far out in the river, put his cigarettes under his hat, pull it firmly down, and start into the current. Captured by the scene, Norman sits down next to his father, and the Reverend reaches a hand out to pat him, but misses. He has to turn his eyes away from Paul's drama and make the act of touching deliberate. He does so, patting Norman gently, looking shyly up into his eyes. Then both men turn away, moved and embarrassed, concentrating on Paul who has begun to swing his right arm back and forth, his eyes fixed firmly on the rock.

REVEREND

No small one for his last one.

[178]

NORMAN *(smiling)*

Never.

Paul's arm begins to swing with perfect rhythm, between ten and two o'clock, again and again. Finally, the line whips out, sailing, catching the sunlight. And then Paul is immobile. The rod points to ten o'clock and ten o'clock points at the rock outcropping. Norman and the Reverend hold their breaths. Then the rod jumps convulsively. Paul's left hand works frantically, trying to feed line to something very big and very powerful. Suddenly, a huge, glittering fish leaps out of the water.

NORMAN

There . . . !

REVEREND

Good Lord . . . !

Paul leans back and the seemingly disconnected fish topples into the water. The rod leaps again with convulsions. Paul's left hand feeds more line.

   His feet scrabble at the loose, treacherous stones beneath the water. He teeters, losing his balance. In order to recover he must let the powerful fish go. But the Reverend knows him well. Smiling, he says:

REVEREND

He'll swim it.

And Paul falls in, dragged downstream by the current and the fish, his expression without fear or excitement, only total concentration. The river pulls him under, pounds him against its rocks, but he refuses to let go—all alone, foolish, courageous. It is Paul summed up and the two men laugh, thrilled as they watch him pass by, until he finds his footing and begins reeling the tired fish in.

   Then the rod convulses and he thrashes forward, surprised, fighting the unseen fish, and Norman yells joyfully:

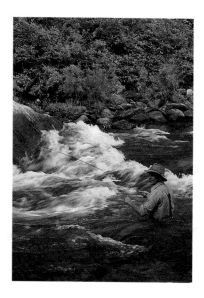

Paul.

NORMAN

The son of a bitch still has *fight!*

He realizes he has sworn in front of his father. But the Reverend only smiles, shaking his head in wonder at the scene before him. Paul raises the rod very high, and with a swift and sure motion, he skids the fish onto a sandbar. Warily, he reaches out and grabs hold of it, then raises the fish. The two men hood their eyes but Paul is too far away to see clearly. Understanding, he splashes through the shallows and runs up the bank, water flying off him, making a rainbow in the sun. Panting, he stops above the other two, dripping on them, grinning, holding the fish up, amazed himself at the ancient behemoth in his hand. Shyly, the Reverend turns partly away and says:

REVEREND

You are a fine fisherman.

PAUL *(equally shy)*

I'm pretty good, but I need three more years before I can think like a fish . . .

The others smile and Norman speaks up, pulling out his Kodak.

NORMAN

Pictures. We need pictures . . .

And he snaps a picture of Paul holding up his fish, drops of water running down his face, his smile simple and pure, and the Narrator begins.

NARRATOR

At that moment I knew, surely and clearly, that I was witnessing perfection. My brother stood before us not on a bank of the Big Blackfoot River, but suspended above the earth, free from all its laws, like a work of art. And I knew just as surely and just as clearly that life is not a work of art, and that the moment could not last.

Norman leaves the police station.

106. EXT. THE POLICE STATION—DAWN. Norman's car stops in front of the station. Norman gets out and hurries up the steps, his face creased with sleep.

NARRATOR

And so, when the police sergeant awakened me next May just at daybreak, I rose and asked no questions.

107. EXT. THE RIVER—EARLY MORNING. The car drives along the shimmering river, out of town.

NARRATOR

I drove home down the length of the river to tell my father and mother that Paul had been beaten to death by the butt of a revolver and his body dumped in an alley.

108. EXT. THE MANSE—DAY. Norman enters the front door as a police car pulls away.

109. INT. THE MANSE—DAY. The Reverend and Mother stand as in a still photo, wearing robes and stunned expressions, incapable of grasping the message. Then, abruptly, Mother turns and walks up the stairs. Norman and the Reverend watch her disappear, wait to hear a door close.

NARRATOR

Without speaking, my mother turned and went to her bedroom where, in a houseful of men and rods and rifles, she had faced most of her great problems alone.

The two men finally turn away from the staircase. The Reverend stands another moment, blank, then asks quietly:

REVEREND

Is there anything else you can tell me?

Norman tries to think. Then he remembers.

NORMAN

Nearly all the bones in his hand were broken.

The Reverend nods thoughtfully and starts without knowing it toward his study. Norman watches, heartbroken, unable to help. Then his father stops and turns back.

REVEREND

Which hand?

Norman holds up a fist.

The Reverend Maclean.

NORMAN

His right hand.

The Reverend nods and starts in his study, but he checks himself and walks slowly upstairs to comfort his wife.

110. INT. THE MANSE—DAY—MONTAGE. As the Narrator continues, the Reverend putters around the house, looking suddenly older. He works in the study. He eats dinner with Mother, neither speaking. He does a small piece of carpentry, working deliberately, silently.

During the next few months my father struggled for more to hold onto, asking me again and again, had I told him everything. And I'd answer, "Everything." And he'd ask, "But isn't there *anything* else you know?" And finally I said to him, "Maybe all I really know about Paul is that he was a fine fisherman." "You know more than that," my father said. "He was beautiful." And that was the last we ever spoke of my brother's death.

111. EXT. THE CHURCH—DAY. A CHURCH BELL *sounds.*

NARRATOR

Indirectly, though, Paul was always present in my father's thoughts.

112. INT. THE CHURCH—DAY.

NARRATOR

I remember the last sermon I heard my father give, not long before his own death.

The Maclean family sit in their usual pew, Mother, old and gray, older Norman and Jessie, and their two small children. At the pulpit stands the Reverend, slight and not as straight, his hair pure white. But his voice is still elegant and moving:

Jessie in church with Clara and children Jean and John.

REVEREND

Each one of us here today will, at one time in our lives, look upon a loved one in need and ask the same question. Thus my text for today—"We are willing, Lord, but what, if anything, is needed?" For it is true that we can seldom help those closest to us. Either we don't know what part of our*selves* to give, or more often than not, the part we have to give . . . is not wanted. And so it is those we live with and *should* know, who elude us.

   (adamant, moved) But we can *still* love them.

It is this next section that speaks the loudest to Norman.

REVEREND

We can love—completely—even without complete understanding . . .

Norman listens intently, moved.

Norman Maclean, 1975.

113. INT. THE MANSE—DAY. On one wall is a gallery of pictures—grandparents, father, Mother, Paul and Norman as children, teens, graduates, and finally the last picture of Paul, holding up the fish, perfect, suspended in time. The sermon fades away as the Narrator begins.

NARRATOR

Now, nearly all those I loved and did not understand in my youth, are dead, even Jessie. But I still reach out to them.

114. EXT. THE RIVER—PRESENT—DAY. Norman, the old man, stands at the shore, casting.

NARRATOR

Of course, now I am too old to be much of a fisherman, and now of course, I usually fish the big waters alone, although some friends think I shouldn't. But, when I am alone in the half-light of the canyon, all existence seems to fade to a being with my soul and memories and the sounds of the Big Blackfoot River, and a four-count rhythm and the hope that a fish will rise.

Eventually, all things merge into one, and a river runs through it. The river was cut by the world's great flood and runs over rocks from the basement of time. On some of the rocks are timeless raindrops. Under the rocks are the words. And some of the words are theirs.

I am haunted by waters.

Fade Out.

THE END